Catching Big Trout

Alan Pearson

Stanley Paul, London

Stanley Paul & Co. Ltd
3 Fitzroy Square, London W1P 6JD

An imprint of the Hutchinson Publishing Group

London Melbourne Sydney Auckland
Wellington Johannesburg and agencies
throughout the world

First published 1979
© Alan Pearson 1979

Set in VIP Times by Input Typesetting Ltd

Printed in Great Britain by The Anchor Press Ltd
and bound by Wm Brendon & Sons Ltd,
both of Tiptree, Essex

British Library Cataloguing in Publication Data
Pearson, Alan
    Catching big trout
    1. Trout fishing
    I. Title
    799.1'7'55   SH687

ISBN 0 09 139790 1 cased
       0 09 139791 X paper

Frontispiece: left top to bottom: Pearson's Green Beast, Grizzly Beetle,
Black Buzzer, Church's Jack Frost
Centre: Orange Buzzer, Walker's Short DFM Green Partridge
Right: Walker's Mayfly Nymph, Daddy Long-legs, Walker's Leaded Shrimp,
Walker's Damselfly Nymph

To Sam Holland, since without his application and determination, really big trout would have remained in the UK an abstract concept.

Also, to Roy Ward, Richard Walker, Tim Daniels, Bob Church, Don Griggs and Richard Gill, each of whom in his own special way has contributed greatly to my successful enjoyment of this specialized branch of the greatest sport of all.

Contents

Specimen Award

This is to certify that

Alan Pearson

caught by fair angling using rod, reel & line

a Tiger Trout. Hybrid(Salmo trutta & Salvelinus
Fontinalis) weighing 1.o77 kg. from Church Hill
Farm Fishery, on the 17th. May,1978

using the following ABU tackle

Delta 3 reel & Abulon

Witnesses to the capture & weighing

D. Robinson & D. Griggs

Signed for and on behalf of ABU (Great Britain) Limited:

Secretary   Managing Director

Certificate of
Recognition For A
World Record
ANGLING ACHIEVEMENT

Alan Pearson
CAUGHT A

19 LBS.   **8** OZS.

all tackle — Division   *Rainbow Trout* — SPECIES

World Records Secretary

Line Class   **May 25, 1977** DATE

Executive Officer
Fishing Hall of Fame

FRESHWATER RECORD

SPECIES BROOK CHARR (BROOK TROUT)
(Salvelinus fontinalis).

WEIGHT FOUR POUNDS EIGHT OUNCES EIGHT DRAMS.

PLACE AVINGTON FISHERY, HAMPSHIRE.

DATE 25TH AUGUST, 1978.

ALAN PEARSON.

THIS IS TO CERTIFY THAT THE
ABOVE NAMED HOLDS THE RECORD
FOR THE LARGEST ROD-CAUGHT
SPECIMEN OF THE ABOVE SPECIES
EVER CAUGHT IN GREAT BRITAIN
AT THE DATE OF CAPTURE

CHAIRMAN

SECRETARY
5 COWGATE, PETERBOROUGH, PE1 1LR

Acknowledgements

The author and publisher wish to acknowledge the use of copyright photographs as follows:

Richard Gill, pages 21, 22, 43, 106, 107
Bill Goddard, pages 77, 82, 90, 92, 95, 108, 120, 123, 133
Stuart Linnell, page 121
Anglers Mail, pages 129, 134

Preface

by Richard Walker

Despite the claims by people who have never caught them that very large trout are easy to catch, there can be few anglers who would not be pleased to land such a fish. In practice this is seldom achieved by using ordinary fly-fishing methods at random, but by deliberately setting out to accomplish it.

At the time of writing, Alan Pearson has landed more trout over 10 pounds in weight than any other British angler. I have myself watched him catch three of them and it is clear that he knows how to do it, the most important qualification for advising others. I have caught enough trout between 8 and 18 pounds to know something of the successful methods and also of the difficulties, all of which are set out very clearly in Pearson's book.

Most of these big fish caught in Southern England are artificially reared and turned loose in angling waters. This is alleged by some to produce fish that are easily hooked and easily landed. Having in my life-time caught a good many naturally bred and naturally fed trout between 5 and 12 pounds, I cannot detect any difference in either their discriminatory or their fighting powers. The only difference is that there are, nowadays, more opportunities to fish for artificially produced trout.

Such considerations are, however, not uppermost in the mind of an angler who is clutching a light trout rod and watching a huge fish, sixty or seventy yards away, going at full speed and appearing unlikely to stop.

Catching fish of that kind, no matter what their origin, is a testing as well as a most exciting business. Alan Pearson's advice is certain to help more anglers to enjoy it.

Evening rise on Dogleg Lake

1 Introduction

I am totally obsessed by trout.

This is not, on the face of it, a remarkable state of affairs, because many anglers seem to share that obsession. On the other hand, there is the difference that my preoccupation is with big trout. Not just any old big trout, but specifically big rainbow trout. It may be thought that there is little difference between one rainbow trout and another, irrespective of their relative sizes, but this makes as much sense as saying that there is no difference between large and small fish of any species, and I think that the specialist seekers after big carp would be very ready and willing to dispute such dubious assertions. I believe that it is difficult to catch big rainbow trout, not the least because of their quite extraordinary strength and cunning, and I would rather take one such rainbow in excess of 10 pounds than two hundred averaging 1 pound each.

I do not expect the majority of people to share my obsession, or even to understand it, but I do believe that there are those who would be very willing indeed to attempt the capture of above-average specimens from waters where they are known to exist, even if such exploits only formed one facet of their whole approach to angling. Indeed, if one considers that the Avington Trout Fishery and the Church Hill Farm Trout Fishery between them are visited by more than 5000 anglers in a season, and that the main attraction of these fisheries is that they hold very large rainbow trout in reasonable numbers; then it has to be the case that the majority of visitors are attracted by the hope – dare I say, the vain hope – that they will succeed in the capture of one of the giants.

Hopes are usually vain because the average angler fails to realize that large and small rainbows are quite different fish, behaving in different ways, and requiring entirely different approaches, both in mental and physical terms. Of course, one of the charms of angling is that anyone *can* be lucky enough to land fish of quite extraordinary dimensions, but luck is a fickle goddess, and the fact is – unpalatable though it may be – that relatively few large rainbow trout are landed by the majority of anglers, while the minority (and a small minority it is) seem somehow or other to catch them with some regularity. Luck does play its part of course, because although one's whole angling operation may be conducted on carefully planned scientific lines, the actual weight of any trout that is landed is very much an imponderable, in that it may, or may not be as large as one hoped. Still, I am not so blasé that I would ignore an estimated 12-pounder because I wanted something bigger, although I would most certainly ignore a 4- or 5-pounder. These days, to be honest, I would also tend to ignore 7- and 8-pounders, unless I had reached the 'last cast' point of no return.

Perhaps this raises the doubt as to what exactly I mean by 'big' rainbows. The term ought to be relative. If a water is stocked mainly with pound fish, then anything over that weight is big in comparison. I confess that I am not interested in relativity, and I now settle on 10 pounds as the minimum weight for my personal definition of a big rainbow, and anything of lesser size can be 'beautiful', or 'magnificent' or 'super', but not 'big'. The distinction is arbitrary, perhaps controversial, and I do not expect many people to agree with me, any more than I expect many people to be capable of catching rainbows of 10 pounds or more in weight. Still, they are there to be caught, and can be caught, provided that one knows what one is doing.

It is my hope that this book, based on my wide experience of catching very big trout over a period of more than a few years, will at least assist the individual angler towards the development of his own personal expertise. At least he can be assured that my concepts are viable and can form a sound foundation to this end.

New trout fisheries and new tackle

It may be recalled that the weight of the rainbow caught at Blagdon, and which held the British record for a good many years, was just 8½ pounds. A rainbow of this size is still worthy of note, but that old record has been broken repeatedly, sometimes more than once in each season, until the present record now stands at exactly 11 pounds more than the old record. This new record was established by a trout that I caught in May 1977, having previously caught one that set a new record in April of the same year, and having it broken again less than a week later. I am persistent, if nothing else!

Obviously times have changed in the trout world, and in recent years there has been a veritable revolution. We have seen the opening, first of all, of a whole series of vast new trout fisheries, in the form of reservoirs, at most of which it is possible to purchase a day ticket permitting the angler to catch up to eight trout, and this at low cost.

At the same time, there has been a quite extraordinary series of advances in tackle design. Rods of hollow glass fibre to suit a variety of purposes are now freely available quite cheaply; carbon-fibre rods, whilst much more expensive, are achieving considerable market penetration; the more traditional built cane rods can also be obtained with ease, and seem less expensive than hitherto – possibly in comparison with carbon-fibre prices. Undoubtedly, other new materials will be used for rod construction – perhaps boron will be next – and will offer certain advantages in use which may be significant enough to offset the undoubted disadvantages that will be inherent.

Reels too have undergone the development process. Standard single-action reels are available in new alloys, or even in carbon fibre, which renders them much lighter than many of their predecessors. A new generation of geared reels is available, enabling a very fast pick-up of loose line, and there are even so-called automatic reels which, by means of a clockwork mechanism, spin merrily away at the press of a lever. I hope it will not seem ungracious if I express the view that I'd just as soon fish with a clockwork orange.

Plastic-covered lines are now the norm, and there is such proliferation of profiles, densities, sizes and alleged end usages that it takes a wise man to find his way through the jungle. It seems that the range is still not wide enough for some of the advanced thinking practitioners of the art, and I read of techniques for the amateur to splice various bits and pieces together in order to construct lines that will float or sink at a whole range of points along the 'business-end'. I sometimes wonder whether there is not far too much change just for the sake of change, and whether any fewer trout would be caught if there was an overnight obliteration of some of the more complex lines.

I wonder, too, whether the world has not turned silly in respect of artificial flies, and in particular, lures. There are so many lures now available that it really does not seem necessary to 'invent' more, and yet every week sees the introduction of yet another. All one has to do, it appears, is take an existing lure and change the colour of some of the dressing materials, give it a new name, and hey presto! another 'killer lure' is born. The fact of the matter is that most of these lures are used in reservoirs where the stock fish tend to be small and incredibly naive, and could be caught as easily on a piece of rag tied to a hook, just as long as it was dragged through the water quickly enough.

Undoubtedly, the development of reservoir fishing, and the introduction of the very wide range of new tackle, coupled with the massive intervention of the angling press, has induced an extremely rapid growth of interest in trout-fishing, and the demand for fishing space is higher now than at any time in the past.

As a direct result of this, we have seen and are still seeing, a high rate of growth in the construction of new trout fisheries, usually small, usually still-water and usually privately owned. Some of them are quite magnificent, delightfully landscaped and possessing high-quality water, while others can be as unattractive as bomb craters, and yet they all tend to have one thing in common: a day ticket on a small private fishery tends to be much more expensive than that obtainable from a water-authority reservoir. The reason for this is quite straightforward. Reservoirs, in general, are not required to make a profit, whereas the private individual cannot consider incurring the capital cost of creating and stocking a fishery, and providing necessary facilities, unless there is the opportunity to recover his costs and compensate for the interest he would have received had that capital sum been invested.

Obviously, the small still-water fisheries have to offer rather more to the angler than do reservoirs, if they are to attract enough custom, so the general tendency is to offer a much higher stocking rate, normally based on high-frequency put-and-take principles, and usually, larger stock is used than in reservoirs.

Catch rate data is readily available, and a fairly standard reservoir analysis shows that even with an eight-fish bag limit, the average catch is 1.1 trout weighing 1.1 pounds per angler per day. A high-cost small fishery often imposes a four-fish limit, and end-of-season analysis usually reveals a catch of about three fish averaging between 2 and 3 pounds, per rod per day. So, at Grafham for example, if you conform to averages, you may catch one trout on each visit, which may probably weigh about 18 ounces. At the other extreme, an expensive day at Church Hill Farm at Mursley, or Avington, near Winchester, may provide you with three trout weighing in total somewhere between 7 and 20 pounds. There is also the strong possibility at either of the two latter fisheries of hooking into a trout weighing 10 or more pounds, and in the case of Avington, even the chance of catching a trout weighing an incredible 20 pounds or more. And there are numerous other small fisheries which contain double-figure trout, as well as plenty in the 7- to 9-pound bracket.

Perhaps this is the most exciting development in the trout-fishing scene; the fact that there are now large numbers of trout around which are of extraordinarily large size, and it may be of interest to consider how this has come about.

In the big reservoirs, there are always trout which remain uncaught at the end of each season, and these are described as 'residuals'. Provided that they are able to survive the traumas of the spawning cycle, the hen fish may well continue to grow and reach excellent weights.

Because of the rather poor quality of stock introduced by most reservoirs, the ultimate top weight is unlikely to exceed 10 pounds, and only a very small percentage of residuals are capable of achieving this. So, in a vast acreage of water, there may be a population density of extra-large rainbows of no more than one trout to five or more acres of water. Occasionally one is caught, usually by the technique of trolling an enormous lure on a lead-cored line, but the dedicated fly fisherman may well feel that this has very little to do with fly-fishing. Frankly I cannot think of a more boring way to spend the day than sitting in a boat, trailing a great lure around, hour after hour after hour. There is no sort of control over what you catch, if anything at all, and the required degree of skill is minimal. However, when a big rainbow is caught, it naturally arouses interest, because to be brutally frank, trout farmers in this country have tended never to exploit the high growth rate, and growth potential, of rainbow trout.

In America, there are fully accredited records of rainbow trout of between 40 and 60 pounds taken in nets, and information has been received from many other parts of the world of wild rainbows into the teens and twenties of pounds.

When a trout is capable of this sort of growth in the wild, it is a source for concern that some trout farmers in this country may have debased the original strain to the extent that it has been virtually impossible for some strains to exceed 5 pounds in weight by the end of their life cycle. One can understand how it happens though. If you hatch a batch of ova, the fry will not exhibit homogeneity of growth. A smallish percentage will grow quite quickly, the majority will grow at a slower rate, another percentage will grow very slowly, and some will fail to make very much growth at all. It has been standard practice for the fish to be sold as they reach a designated size, so obviously the faster-growers are sold first, the medium-growers next, and the slow-growers tend to be retained as brood stock. These pass on to their progeny an enhanced tendency to grow at a slow rate, and in the end much available stock grows very slowly indeed, in comparison with the original norm of the species.

The Avington Strain

It would seem a simple enough matter to reverse this process, and carefully select as brood stock only those rainbows which revealed the desired characteristics of fast growth, good food conversion, and correct physical configuration, and indeed much work of this nature has taken place in America over the past forty years.

No one in this country seemed to be at all interested, until Sam Holland retired from the aerospace industry and settled at Avington. His early work was confined to the re-establishment of a trout fishery, but it was not long before he became dissatisfied with the quality of stock that he was able to purchase, and decided to implement his own selective breeding programme. The results are now common knowledge. He created a new race of rainbow trout, now registered as the 'Avington strain', which are capable of the sort of growth rate exhibited by only the best of the North American wild fish. There have always been a few private fisheries that included some large rainbows in their stockings, but photographic evidence suggests that most of these fish were very old brood stock, well past their prime, black as Satan's armpits, and extremely deficient in the fin department. Suddenly, the picture began to change. Anglers began to catch 7- and 8-pound rainbows at Avington that were only two years old; then came the flood of

Roy Ward (left) and Sam Holland at Avington choosing broodstock for the selective breeding programme

double-figure specimens at three years of age. I know, without any shadow of doubt, that there are rainbows in the fishery up to 30 pounds in weight, in excellent condition, and contrary to popular belief (which is usually incorrect) there is no possibility that they were all introduced at such weights.

Many people believe that big trout require a vast quantity of food to survive, but in the case of good-quality rainbows this is simply untrue. In theory, it takes the same amount of food to grow a rainbow from 1 pound to 2 pounds, as it does to grow another from 20 pounds to 21 pounds. In practice, the larger fish may require slightly less food, because it expends far less energy than the smaller fish, as a result of a highly territorial mode of life. A small rainbow expends a lot of energy in just swimming around, hunting and playing. A big rainbow establishes a domicile with two or three rich feeding grounds in the immediate vicinity, and periodically sets off on an extremely slow feeding trip around these larder

Stripping ova from a ripe Avington rainbow

areas. This does not mean to imply that the big rainbow is not powerful and very fast through the water when need arises; merely that under all normal circumstances there is absolutely no need for haste.

Sam Holland's breeding programme has continued unchecked, and in recent years he has stepped up production quite dramatically, enabling him to sell off surplus stock to other fisheries. This means that quite a number of other small fisheries, and a few reservoirs, are able to claim that they have stocks of Avington-strain rainbows, but it is also true to say that many of them have stock from other sources too. Still, there is no contravention of the basic principle that a growing number of fisheries now contain very large trout as a result of the Avington programme.

On the other hand, reports of captures of big rainbows are still not as frequent as one might expect, but really this is not too difficult to understand. A big rainbow is not at all the same sort of fish as a small rainbow, because with the onset of maturity, it has tended to adopt a different life style. Unless the angler understands this life style, then he really has very little chance of hooking into such a great fish, except by accident. Accidents of this nature are frequently followed by another accident, such as leader breakage, leaving the angler with yet another story of the one that got away.

The importance of tactics

It is my contention that one can set out one's stall to catch these big trout. All one has to do is try to understand the quarry, and be very sure that correct tackle and tactics are employed.

This book purports to explain how big trout may be caught, and my credentials in that respect are probably sound enough. As I write, my personal tally stands at thirty-one trout in excess of 10 pounds taken from British day-ticket fisheries open to all, plus another ten trout within the same classification from waters either in this country, or abroad, which may fairly be said not to be available to the general public. On three occasions I have caught trout heavier than the then record. I have lost count of the numbers of trout that I have taken weighing between, say 7 pounds and 10 pounds – not that I am not proud of such captures, but simply that there have been rather a lot of them in the last few years.

I suppose it would be easy enough for me to use, as my model for this book, any of the fly-fishing instruction manuals published in recent years, which commence with an introduction (as does this), and then follow on with a dissertation on tackle, working through, in that order, rods, reels, lines, leaders, flies, and eventually to tactics. The trouble is that, as I see it, all these matters are inextricably bound together, and one ought to cover them all simultaneously. This hardly seems possible, and I have found it extremely difficult to determine the correct sequence. Flies, for example, ought not to be left until the end of the tackle section, as is normally the case, because it is the specific size of fly selected for use that suggests the strength of leader, and this leader equally dictates the power and action of the rod. And the correct fly to use is nominated by a tactical decision, which in itself requires some knowledge of the behavioural patterns of one's quarry.

After due reflection I am obliged to say that *I believe that tactics are more important than anything else in the pursuit of big rain-bows.*

It is always the good angler who approaches the water correctly, spends whatever time may be necessary in detailed observation and draws the correct conclusion from what he may observe. It is usually the good angler who can overcome the handicap of unsuitable or inefficient tackle, and still land his fish. No matter how very expensive, and well-engineered his tackle may be, the man who does not approach his fishing in the correct tactical manner is the man most unlikely to succeed. Therefore, I give tactics pride of place, and treat everything else as subordinate.

2 Tactics

It is self-evident that for the angler to be successful in his efforts to catch big rainbow trout, he has first of all to be sure that the fishery which he chooses to make the subject of his campaign actually contains enough trout of the appropriate size to make the exercise worthwhile. This is a truth so basic that I would find it difficult to believe that anyone could overlook it, and yet I do know some anglers, vastly experienced in years if nothing else, who have devoted much of their lives to the fruitless pursuit of big fish in a water which may possibly have held some sizeable specimens many years previously, but which now holds only small fish in their millions. There seems to be a blind spot in the reasoning processes of many anglers, perhaps all.

Some autobiography

I recognize this blind spot, because I have experienced it myself. I was born into a family of anglers, educationalists and other eccentrics, and it is hardly surprising that as a toddler my obsessions were centred upon water, fishing tackle and books. The water obsession was easily satisfied, because we lived in a house backing on to the River Thames at Old Isleworth. At least, we lived there until the continual struggle to preserve me from a watery grave became too much, and we moved to another house about a mile from the river. Life then became much simpler for my parents, for should I disappear from view for longer than two minutes, they merely sent a search party to intercept me as I toddled on chubby legs along the shortest route to my beloved river.

There was always fishing tackle around, and since I treated it with great reverence, it was never forbidden to me, and as I recall, I usually found it simpler to assemble a rod and reel than tie my shoelaces. Books abounded, and by means I do not remember, I was taught to read at a very early age, certainly long before I first attended school at five years of age. Indeed, by that time, family legend has it that I was reading novels. Be that as it may, there is no doubt that I was reading books on angling by such authors as Bickerdyke, Francis Francis and Jardine, and trying to relate my understanding of their contents to the actual expeditions to the river with my grandfather and uncles, who were dedicated anglers. The books that I enjoyed most were those dealing with trout-fishing, although I failed totally to comprehend the technicalities of that branch of the sport, and my first attempts at fly-fishing involved the suspension of a fly beneath my float. Oddly enough, I did catch some fine fat dace like that!

Eventually the penny dropped, and by the age of about seven, I possessed a fly rod constructed from greenheart split down from the butt of an old Castle Connell salmon-fly rod, and armed with a wooden centre-pin reel loaded with level flax line. My favourite venue was Syon Reach at low tide, and for years I used to fish there, flogging the water furiously with a team of three wet flies, and catching a fair number of dace and roach, with an occasional chub to liven things up. Never a trout, though. Frankly, there were no trout there to be caught, and I knew this as well as anyone, but since there was no trout-fishing available to me elsewhere, I kept on fishing in the hope that I might experience a small miracle. I never did, but my enthusiasm was undampened. That is what I mean by a blind spot. I knew there were no trout there to be caught, but I never let such a minor detail distract me from my trout-fishing expeditions.

Oddly enough, my earliest encounters with trout were on the dear old Thames, and I think that my experiences there have had considerable impact on my whole approach to fishing for big trout. Of course, it is usually a waste of time to attempt catching Thames trout on a fly, although I have taken a few in that way, and the time-honoured techniques involved the presentation of a live min-now, gudgeon or bleak on float tackle, or spinning a natural dead-bait, in the sort of areas that these wondrous creatures were alleged to inhabit. And, every now and again, the earth shook, a trout took the bait and even more rarely came to the net.

Over the years it dawned on me that there had to be a more efficient way to fish for trout than just offering a bait in reputed holding areas which were possibly innocent of any sort of fish, and

I began to spend more and more time in observation, and less and less time in actual fishing. Remarkably enough, my catch rate improved, because I was now actually locating the whereabouts of my quarry before I deigned to offer it a bait. This is not quite as easy as it seems in water as turbid as the Thames, but I learned to recognize a true holding area, and wait patiently for some sign that it was inhabited. Gratifying though all this was, I was still not doing what I wanted to do, which was catch trout on the fly.

Then came the Grafham opening, and what a revelation this was. At last I could *afford* to go fly-fishing, and with every expectation of catching trout. Unfortunately, before I could achieve much benefit from the changing circumstances, I was smitten with a rather unpleasant affliction which caused a seizing-up of my arms, and required me to be clad in an iron maiden of a corset in order that my spine should not collapse. It was tough enough to get about in that fearful contraption of canvas and iron, and casting a fly was impossible. It was as much as I could do to manage a coarse-fishing session of a couple of hours. I dare say that if I had been truly dedicated, I would have taught myself to cast with my toes or my teeth, but I just waited patiently until some sort of a cure was effected, and then, very slowly, I overcame the problems and began casting a fly once more.

Standard reservoir tactics even then were to cast out a lure as far as possible, and drag it back fast, and since everyone was going through these motions, there was little point in attempting to fish a nymph at close quarters. No way would there be a trout within thirty yards of the bank by the time the monstrous regiment of lure-flashers had marched forward in unison until the water was lapping the tops of their waders. Perhaps there was an element of sour grapes in my attitude, because for a considerable time I was unable to control my casting action sufficiently to be able to put a long line out, and I could not fish for long without requiring to rest.

Then I discovered that fishing from a boat at Grafham was very much easier for me, because enough trout would rise within casting distance for me to cover a fair number, and my catch rate increased appreciably. The thing I did not care for was that these stock trout were generally so small that I felt guilty about keeping them. You have to remember that I had spent years catching trout to Thames size limits, and these small stockies seemed too innocent, too vulnerable, for me to take too much pleasure in catching them.

I began to extend my sphere of operations. I spent time at Packington, which I thoroughly enjoyed because in the smaller lakes I found it easier to locate my trout first, and then make the decision as to whether I would fish for it or not. I visited Draycote Water many times during the opening season, and found that there too I could be rather more selective, to the extent that I caught the biggest rainbow of that first season, and was duly awarded a reel. I have to confess that it seemed like false pretences to accept a prize for catching a trout of less than 3 pounds!

Around this time I gained fishing rights on two small chalkstreams, not far from my home, and at last I began really to enjoy my fishing. Now I could creep and crawl through the undergrowth to my heart's content, spy on the trout in their natural environment, opt to fish for a trout that I could actually see, and watch the whole sequence of events from start to finish. My catch rate improved by leaps and bounds, and the average weight showed similar improvement to the point where I actually expected to catch at least one 3- to 4-pounder on every excursion. I could not help but think that in a more extensive water, the trout might have been larger, and yet I was rapidly coming to the conclusion that all reservoirs, even the smallest, were too big for me to fish in the way that I wanted to.

Then a sequence of events occurred that totally changed my life. Firstly, I hooked a terrifyingly large trout at Grafham, which I played out and eventually lost through a mishap. I still do not care to estimate the size of that trout, but I have always been convinced that it would have exceeded the British record by a very hefty margin. Secondly, I gave up my career as an executive with a very large industrial organization to become a trout-farmer and freelance fishery and fish-farming consultant, a major change in direction for me, although I had been providing an advisory service to fisheries for some years.

My first important assignment as a consultant was in Ethiopia, where my task was to survey the sporting potential of the extensive system of lakes and rivers in that delightful and unique country. My fate was sealed when, in the Bale Mountains, I succeeded in catching rainbow trout the like of which I had never dreamed could exist – and the brown trout were also superb, although not so large. All these trout had been introduced as fry, imported from Kenya, and the rainbows had settled in with apparent ease, grow-

ing to extraordinary size and becoming a self-maintaining population. These were river trout, and since the rivers were rather larger
than my little chalk-streams with frequent deep pools where flow
rate was, at that time, very slow, I found myself fishing what were
to all intents and purposes, small still-waters.

Shortly after my return to Britain, I met Sam Holland for the
first time, and became very interested in his operation. I was so
impressed by the great progress that he had made with his selective
breeding programme, that I purchased all my basic stock requirements from him for my own farm, and this gave me the most
wonderful opportunity to study the behaviour patterns of the
larger fish. I do mean larger, because at one time during the first
year I had ponds stocked with rainbows up to and over 18 pounds
in weight, while the rod-caught record stood some 4 or 5 pounds
less than that. Also I was spending as much time as I could conveniently spare at Avington, nominally fishing, but probably
spending much more of my time in observing the fishery, the
behaviour of the trout, and equally important, the tactics of the
other anglers present.

You may feel that this prolonged digression, this autobiographi-
cal survey, has very little to do with tactics. In a sense you may be
right, but the point I am trying to establish is that the tactics for
catching big rainbows were not revealed to me in a blinding flash,
or presented to me carved on clay tablets whilst I was on the Bale
Mountains. The tactics I now invariably employ have been
developed over the course of many years, and relate to myriad
experiences in many places, doing many different things. So let us
now consider what these tactics are, how one actually sets about
the problem of catching a big rainbow trout.

Reconnaissance: finding the hot-spots

As I said at the beginning of this chapter, it is first necessary to
select a fishery well known to hold big trout in fair numbers, and a
careful perusal of angling publications will soon indicate an appropriate venue. Having selected your fishery, make up your mind
that unless you find the environment distasteful, you will concentrate on that fishery, and that fishery alone, until your first objective is achieved – the capture of your first big trout. Bob Church
claims that I know every blade of bankside grass, every pebble on

the bed, and every leaf of every submerged aquatic plant at the fisheries I spend most time visiting. This is an exaggeration, albeit a flattering one, but it does underline the necessity to know the main features of the battleground.

It may seem a waste of money to pay to visit a fishery, and then spend most of your time studying the environment, but in the early stages there is little option. Fortunately, most of the fisheries that hold big trout possess clear water for much of the season, and with the aid of polarised spectacles it will be easy enough for you to distinguish detail beneath the surface.

The first objective is to gain an overall impression of the fishery. How deep are the deepest holes, how shallow are the shallows? Of what is the bed composed, what are the main varieties of submerged and emergent aquatic plants, what natural food forms can you distinguish? Can you see the trout? If so, how large are they, and what are they doing? If you can find an area where the water is at least three or four feet deep, with weedbeds or other cover close at hand, station yourself on the bank as unobtrusively as possible, and just wait and watch. If you wait long enough, you may well see trout moving in and out of this potential feeding area, but if you can resist the temptation to try your luck with a cast or two, you will be well advised to do so. Spend most of your day in this fashion, then – and only then – try catching a fish to avoid the blank.

Believe me, it will take several such reconnaissance trips before you begin, even remotely, to understand the fishery. Slowly, the pieces will click into place, and you will learn to recognize the areas where fish will always appear at some time or other during the day. You will begin to notice that the trout which are swimming fairly quickly are not feeding at all, and you would be wasting your time if you were to cast to one of these. You will see that the feeding trout are the slow cruisers, and that the bigger they are, the less likely they will be to do other than cruise slowly, taking food items which are very close to their noses, and very rarely diverging from their pre-selected route to take titbits which are not within sucking-in distance. Also, it will eventually become obvious to you that these bigger trout have their set routes, and will usually move from one feeding area to another in strict rotation, following a similar route each time they make the circuit. You may not be able to discern, to your complete satisfaction, the exact location of their rest point, the specific territorial lurking place where they digest their latest food intake before commencing the circuit once more. This is not really of great significance, since you would be extremely lucky if you could drop a fly anywhere near them, and even if you could it is unlikely that it would be taken. It seems that there is a clear distinction between feeding areas and resting areas.

One factor may have become obvious to you already. It is not unusual for the patrol circuit to take place fairly close to the bank – indeed, if this were not so, you would probably be unable to see your quarry at all. I do not doubt that similar patrolling activities do take place in the deeper water, out of sight, but attempting to catch a hypothetical trout while it is undertaking a hypothetical feeding patrol is a total waste of time. Occasionally a big trout is hooked by the speculative prospecting of unseen depths, but this can only be classified as an improbable accident, and very few trout hooked like this are ever landed.

So let us assume that the big trout has been observed, and its patrol area identified. Now you have to decide upon two other important factors. Firstly, how deep is it swimming? In other words, at what depth is it feeding? Secondly, what is it feeding on? It sounds simple enough, does it not, to decide upon the swimming depth of an observed fish? Yet, I have seen experienced anglers sum up such a situation by deciding that the trout weighs 6 pounds and is swimming at a depth of three feet, whereas the truth of the matter is that the brute weighs something more than 12 pounds and is six feet below the surface.

This is another good reason for familiarizing oneself with the fishery, because vision can be seriously affected by water quality. At Avington, and at Church Hill Farm, the water is exceptionally alkaline, and creates the effect of reducing the size of an observed fish and appearing to bring it much closer to the surface than in fact is the case. At Crown Netherall Trout Fishery, the reverse appears to be true and an observed trout seems to be deeper in the water than it really is, but there is no visual interference with actual size. So what you have to do is develop your own built-in compensation device which corrects your vision, and gives you the true readings of depth and size. Practice alone will assist in this function.

Wherever possible the effort must be made to establish what natural insects the trout is feeding on. All mature trout are, to some extent, capable of the pre-occupation which induces them to feed upon one life form exclusively for irregular periods of time, and in such case it is often quite pointless in offering an imitation of anything else, even to the extent that shape and colour may be perfect, but if the size is wrong then it will be rejected.

I have already indicated that big trout are very unwilling to make more than a minor diversion from their chosen route in order to ingest even the choicest of morsels, and this is why you have to determine swimming depth accurately. It is essential that, by the time the trout reaches your offering, it is in exactly the right position to be sucked in without any difficulty. If you visualize a spot about three inches in front of the trout's mouth, and in the same plane, then your fly should preferably lie somewhere within the arc extending no more than three inches on either side of that point. An exact imitation of the preferred food item may assist in inducing the take.

Of course, this is an extremely difficult level of accuracy to achieve, and requires an intimate knowledge of the sinking rate of each and every one of your fly patterns. You may find it convenient to use leaded dressings where your quarry is a deep cruiser, and deliberately cast beyond the point you are aiming at. Then, as your fly sinks, allow it to reach a slightly greater depth than necessary, and at the appropriate time, draw it towards you, and up, until it reaches the defined area at the same moment as the trout. This frequently results in an 'induced take'.

If your quarry is a shallow cruiser, it is often a simple matter to put your fly into the correct place, with sinking depth readily controllable by greasing the leader to within the correct distance from the fly. It may be easier to determine upon what the trout is feeding when it is close to the surface, but it should not be forgotten that the angler is also that much more visible to the fish.

I have often noticed that the biggest trout in a river fishery are so very certain of their ability to evade capture, that they seem to take almost no notice of anglers, ignoring them as they walk – or creep – along the bank, and carefully spurning even the most succulent looking fly, no matter how well presented, if it is attached to a leader. They know all about poor fools of anglers, and tend to ignore them.

It is much the same with the giant trout of a small still-water fishery. They will tolerate a splashy cast, a badly presented fly, and merely shrug their hefty shoulders in a resigned fashion before

Feeding patrol – large rainbow taking chironomid pupae just subsurface

aiming a sneer in the general direction of the angler and gently cruising on. This infuriating cocksureness can drive an angler insane, but it also gives him more than one chance at a fish, for that arrogant brute is not going to change his life style just because of an idiot messing about on the bank.

What can cause panic amongst trout of any size is noise, and the flashing of reflected light. I will come back to the reflected light problems in the section dealing with tackle, but noise – or the lack of it – has tactical implications. There are well-meaning people who will tell you that fish cannot hear noises, that noise does not transmit readily through water, and it is quite in order to shout, sing, play transistor radios and give vent to earsplitting whistles, just as long as earth-stamping vibration is avoided. The truth of the matter is this. Sound travels through water four times as fast as it does through air. Sound waves in water, though having only one-sixtieth of the displacement amplitude of the same sound waves in air, have sixty times the pressure amplitude. Also, the absorption, or attenuation of sound in water is far less than in air. If that seems too highly technical, accept a reasonable simplification as being that sound not only travels four times faster in water than in air, and suffers less diminution, it also exerts sixty times the pressure on the lateral line of the fish than it does on the human eardrum. Still think noise does not matter? The very least effect of noise is to create an awareness in the fish that a large noise-producing entity is fairly close at hand or even at a more remote point on the feeding circuit, and I firmly believe that this increases the odds against the angler.

What do you do when you are unable to discover what it is, if anything, that your observed trout is eating? My opinion is that you offer what appears to be a particularly succulent mouthful. If the fishery is rich in shrimp, then offer a shrimp pattern which is larger and fatter than the natural. Select any natural life form that you know to be present, and offer it larger than life-size.

Sometimes great success can be achieved with sound imitation of life forms that do not exist in the fishery, provided that they appear to have life, and offer a reasonably satisfying mouthful. It is at times such as this that really large dressings of the Mayfly Nymph and Damselfly Nymph can be extremely effective, as can oversize Pheasant-Tail Nymphs. If this fails, perhaps a switch to the other end of the size spectrum is indicated.

All you can do is either sit tight and wait for a feeding pattern to emerge, or run through the various permutations of large, small, bright, drab, and perhaps risk putting the trout down for a while. Every situation needs to be treated on its individual merits, but I do use a very rough and easy guide. If the trout seems to be 'on the fin', by which I mean looking alert, and interested in your offerings, then I would persist in attempting to induce it to accept one fly or another. If, on the other hand, the general impression you receive is of dourness, or even ill-humour, rather like a Scotsman

on his way to kirk on Sunday morning, then just put your tackle
aside for a while.

I do not mean to imply that you should remain in just one
potential hot-spot. As your knowledge of a fishery increases, so
will your register of hot-spots. Some are only fishable when the sun
is hanging in a cloudless sky and there is not a breath of wind.
Others fish best with a westerly, or a southerly wind, or in cloudy
and cool conditions. There are early season hot-spots, mid-season
hot-spots, and a few late season hot-spots.

If it is necessary for you, as an individual, to make the occasional
move, then by all means do so, because you will enjoy your day
more, and probably fish more efficiently as a result. Never expect,
however, that you will eventually be able to return to a favourite
spot temporarily deserted. Almost certainly you will find it
occupied by a red-faced, beer-swilling, thick-necked yahoo, who
scarcely knows one end of his rod from the other and cannot cast
straight to save his life, and who will proudly display to you the
fine, fat, silvery 15-pounder that he has just landed. (I am only
trying to describe the mental reactions you will undoubtedly
experience unless you are a saint. Really, the 'offending' angler
will be a very nice chap and thoroughly efficient, who has been
waiting patiently for you to remove your incompetent self from his
favourite beat before you succeed in putting down every decent
trout for miles around.)

Casting

There is a problem connected with close-quarters fishing, and that
is the difficulty of casting accurately at very close range, when only
a foot or two of line may be extended beyond your rod tip. All that
one can do is practise, and even then, it is not easy. On the other
hand, you have the advantage that when the trout you are trying to
catch is virtually under your rod tip, you enjoy a perfect view of
events. Many anglers fail in their pursuit of big trout because they
are just not single-minded enough, and allow themselves to be
sidetracked into casting at smaller trout than they are really hoping
to catch. This is unbelievably damaging to prospects of success. I
make a practice of cutting my casting down to an absolute
minimum, ignoring lesser trout and not casting to the big ones
unless I am certain that I can put my fly in exactly the right place.

In this context, perhaps I should refer back to my earlier comments on the need to be accurate within the three dimensions indicated by the exact positioning of the fly on the required horizontal plane, and stipulate that you have to be accurate in the fourth dimension as well. This fourth dimension is, of course, time, and it ought to be self-evident that you need more than just the ability to place a fly correctly within the three dimensions. If you fail to be accurate in the fourth dimension, and get the fly there too late, the fish will have passed on, and so will your dream of catching it.

Consider the successful big-game hunter. Whether his quarry is lion, or elephant, or leopard, he has to know a great deal about his quarry. He has to know the preferred environment and feeding habits, and how to stalk the animal so that he can get within reasonable shooting distance. He has to be able to handle his rifles, and know the right one for the task in hand, and, of course he has to be able to contain himself in patience until the opportunity presents itself for a killing shot. He does not loose off volley after volley, whether he can see his prey or not, in the hope that the creature will happen to walk into a high velocity slug. Similarly, I do not cast unless I am sure that my cast is going to tell, that the fly I present will be seen by the trout in very close proximity, and that it has a chance of being taken. It is possible that during an entire twelve-hour day on a fishery, I may only cast a dozen times, but each one of those casts has a purpose.

It may be of advantage to summarize the approach to this point of casting. Firstly, the angler has taken care to visit a fishery known to contain certain large rainbow trout. Secondly, by prolonged visual inspection of the water, he has located his quarry and identified a patrolling area for the particular specimen. Thirdly, he has adapted his vision to the physical characteristics of that fishery in order that he can automatically register in his mind the actual size of the trout and the depth at which it is swimming. Fourthly, he will have studied the fauna of the fishery with care, so that he will always have a pretty good idea of what it is that the trout is likely to be feeding upon at any given time. Lastly, he will have learned to differentiate between the slow-moving but alert fish ready to feed, and the faster-moving or perhaps somnolent trout that is not in feeding mood.

Those large white lips opening . . .

Fighting the trout

The big-game hunter's task is over once he has loosed off his shot.
The angler has only just begun his task with his accurate cast.
When the trout is seen to take the fly, when that large mouth opens
and closes, and your fly has vanished from sight, the hook has
somehow to be set. I lift the rod firmly with one hand, pulling
smartly on the line with the other, thus drawing the hook firmly
home. I do not like the term 'strike', not only for its connotations
of industrial disorder, but also because it appears to have overtones of violence. The action is really a very firm pull, and provided that your hook is sharp, it should set firmly into the trout's
mouth, unless you are so unlucky as to be impeded by the tooth
structure. In this specific situation, heavier striking would not
achieve penetration, just a broken leader. With just a trifle of luck,
the hook will become embedded in gristle, and you are attached to
a very tough opponent indeed.

Once hooked, the trout may react in a variety of ways. If it should set off on a fast run, then I am usually quite confident that it will not take too long before the landing net is brought into operation, in spite of the fact that my rather loose terminology tends to obscure the fact that fast means anything up to 50 m.p.h! A trout that behaves in this manner may be hurt, or it may be scared, but temporarily it loses its natural cunning, and relies upon sheer speed and power to put as much distance as possible between itself and the place in which it was frightened or hurt. The maintenance of maximum strain is essential, and the most efficient application is induced by moving the rod into the horizontal plane, thus applying sidestrain.

Sooner or later the run will peter out, and the trout can be worked back to close quarters. Almost certainly it will then set off on another fast run. Classically, as run succeeds run, the distance covered becomes progressively shorter until in due course the trout is completely exhausted. Sounds simple put like this, but in practice there are quite a few problems. This question of speed, for one thing. I once saw Bob Church hook a big trout just under his rod tip. Before he could react properly, it was fifty yards away, and his line was completely out of the water, from rod tip to trout, in a dead straight line. If his line had snagged, or his reel jammed, that fish would have broken the leader like a piece of rotten thread. I am delighted to say that nothing of the sort happened, and after an exciting battle, Bob netted an enormous trout of 15½ pounds.

When I hook a trout that does not head for the middle distance, then I know I am in for trouble. This will be one of the truly arrogant fish, confident that he is more than a match for any silly little angler, and he behaves accordingly. He cruises casually around, not in any great haste, and resists totally any attempt to induce him to change depth or direction, no matter how much strain is applied at this stage. Before long, a new idea will occur, and the head will go down, pointing away from the angler, and the body lying against the line. The tail then begins to act as a flail, smashing repeatedly against the leader, and imparting a sensation to the rod not unlike it being hit with a club. If this proves to be unsuccessful, then the next gambit will be to attempt to rub the hook out on a convenient gravel patch. If this fails, then there may be a reversion to tail-flailing, or perhaps coming to the surface, facing up the line, and shaking the head from side to side with incredible ferocity.

Provided that the angler can weather all these storms, it may begin to dawn on the trout that it is in trouble, and a different behaviour pattern emerges. Perhaps refuge will be sought in a succession of weed or reed beds. Once a big trout actually succeeds in holing-up in a massive weedbed, reedbed or conglomeration of algae, direct contact between angler and fish is usually lost. Sometimes the situation may be retrieved by hand-lining the trout, plus accumulated weed, out of the danger area, and it does sometimes happen that a mass of weed blinds the fish and restricts its struggles, permitting a simple netting. More often, the loss of contact allows the trout to shed the hook. Usually, the final result is a stalemate, with the trout declining to emerge from refuge, and the angler powerless to induce it to do so. In such case, breakage usually follows, as the frustrated angler continues to work by tugging and heaving on the line.

Perhaps a series of fast runs will develop, with the trout attempting all the earlier gambits at a point now far removed from the angler – who knows? The fight goes on and on, and if the angler is too nervous to apply as much pressure as is needed, or is conscious of the inadequacy of his tackle to stand up to that sort of pressure, then it will be a very long fight indeed. And the longer the fight, the more chance there is of the hook-hold working loose, or the leader giving way at a knot.

Some years ago, I had an object lesson in the playing of big trout that I have never forgotten, and it has coloured my approach ever since. I had access to a private lake, not normally fished by anyone, which contained a very good head of rainbow trout of weights ranging from about 6 pounds up to as much as low double figures. The water was fairly shallow, and extremely weedy, with extensive and well-established water lily beds. I was reasonably successful in landing some of the bigger trout, but too many of them managed to run me into some under-water obstruction or other, and break me.

On one occasion, I managed to gain permission for Richard Walker to accompany me to this lake, and he opted to commence fishing in what could only be described as a hole in a dense lily patch, with just a very narrow channel leading from the bank to this small area of clear water. The reason for selecting this spot was quite evident. There was a very fine trout lying there, obviously in taking mood. I moved further up the bank, and looked back in time to see Walker cast to, and hook the trout, which obviously objected strongly to that indignity. About thirty seconds later, still objecting strenuously, it was in the landing net, being hauled up the bank. It weighed 9½ pounds!

I examined the tackle. Normal fly rod, normal line, light leader – the whole thing seemed quite impossible. I, somewhat awestruck, asked how on earth Walker had managed it. In his usual way, he first of all pointed out all the 'why' factors, which had to do with the strong possibility of losing the trout if it had managed to get into the lily stems, and then followed all the 'hows' which seemed, as I understood it, to relate to the necessity of never allowing the trout its head, of forestalling its every action, and of using its own power against it.

I watched the same exercise undertaken by Walker several times that day, and began to see a glimmering of light at the end of the tunnel. Walker subsequently hooked a rainbow at Avington on 2 April 1976, which was, in his opinion, far too big, far too heavy, for the rather light leader he was using at the time. He remained out of sight of the trout, which was one of the awkward type that prefer a long-drawn-out scrap, and by maintaining constant light pressure induced it to move between two fixed points. It would swim slowly to one, wallow about for a bit, and then return to the other to have another wallow. There is no doubt that it did not know it had been hooked, and was just bewildered by events. On returning to one wallow spot, it discovered far too late that a big landing net had been stealthily introduced, and while it was look-ing at something else, up came the net, and out came the trout. Weight – 18¼ pounds, a new record although never formally claimed.

Once the story got out, quite a few people misunderstood what had actually taken place, and, in trying to turn the whole thing into a joint attack on both Walker and the fighting attributes of big rainbows, merely demonstrated their own ignorance of the subject. A more correct assessment is that Walker used his superb water-craft and knowledge of piscine psychology to outwit a very big fish with which his tackle would not have otherwise been able to cope.

I have never forgotten the lesson of that day, and over the years I have developed my own methods of coping with very big trout, but I am the first to admit that without the advice and help I received from Richard Walker, the story would undoubtedly be very different.

My approach is this. Accepting that a big rainbow is a confident, arrogant creature, fully aware of its own power and speed, then the most sensible approach is to destroy that confidence by continual harassment. Try to forestall every move, try to anticipate and negate every action and reaction. Use every scrap of power that you can transmit through your tackle to turn the trout away from the route it opts to take. Stop a run as quickly as you can, certainly before maximum speed can be achieved. When the tail-flailing is about to start, or has started, use maximum side strain to pull the head round, and the leader out of harm's way. Hang on tight, even if you feel your tackle is close to destruction point, to prevent an obstruction being attained. When the trout tries to rub the hook out on gravel, then if you cannot shift it any other way, pump. Yes, pump, in exactly the same way that you bring a big sea fish up from the depths.

Risky? Of course it is, but at least you are carrying the fight to the trout, and not letting it dictate terms to you. I have no patience with those worthies that stand up straight on the bank, rod tip gently nodding, and the trout doing pretty well as it pleases. You can take twenty minutes to land a 2-pound trout using that technique, and if you try it on a really big fish, the odds are heavily against your landing it.

To kill your trout within safe time limits, you have to work very hard yourself, and the more effort that you expend, the more quickly the trout will come to net. I am not suggesting that you should use heavy tackle – far from it – or that you should take insane risks. Nevertheless, you are in combat with a powerful adversary, and it would be foolish to imagine that all you have to do is just stand there, going through those gently artistic motions that are often believed to be the mark of the true sportsman. Maybe they are, if you are playing a 4-ounce brown trout in a tiny burn, using a 2-pound leader. That may well be part of the mystique of that branch of fly-fishing, but it has nothing at all to do with the efficient capture of a fine sporting fish of very large size.

Wild trout and farmed trout

To catch the very largest rainbows with any degree of regularity, you have first of all to know something about the behavioural patterns and dietary preferences of your quarry; you have to understand the workings of your tackle; and, most important of all, you have to be a tactician in every sense of the word. My whole approach has been developed over a great many years, and no doubt will continue to develop for as long as I am permitted to go on fishing, but I am not suggesting that everyone has to waste as much time as that. This book sets out the basic concepts. If you can take those concepts and adapt them to your own particular approach, then you can catch big trout. I cannot guarantee results if you tamper with the concepts too much, or alter the basic mechanics of the exercise, but then, who can guarantee anything in angling?

One thing that can be guaranteed is that there have been some quite extraordinarily misconceived comments about these big rainbows in the angling press, and that these comments are likely to be repeated every time any publicity is given to the capture of another. You may see big rainbows described as 'silly' or 'tame', 'hand-reared' or 'incapable of putting up a fight' and even that these silly, tame, sloppy trout are deliberately put into a fishery shortly before the arrival of Pearson, Walker, Church, Dobbs, Shrive and Co, in order that they can haul them out with the greatest of ease, and splash them across the press, with maximum publicity thus accruing. In fact, all that these comments reveal is the ignorance of their originators. In order that the uncommitted angler should not be misled, it is worth spending a little time considering the facts.

Because rainbow trout are incapable of natural breeding in the vast majority of waters in this country, it is necessary that the stock required to meet the ever-increasing demand is produced by farming. In fact, brown trout also need to be produced in the same way, not because they cannot breed naturally (although of course they cannot, in many fisheries), but because angling pressures are far too high to permit them to be self-maintaining. Thus, the vast majority of all trout stocks are 'hand-reared' up to the point of their release into the fishery, and if hand-rearing implies tameness, then they are all 'tame'.

The fact is, that the traumas associated with the transference of trout from farm pond to fishery induce a total reliance upon instinct, and a reversion to instinct dominance creates 'wildness'. There may be a significant exception, and this relates to the common practice at reservoirs to have stock introduced in very large

A huge fish going at full speed and unlikely to stop

numbers. Because the trout will have been reared in high-density ponds, and transported in even higher-density tanks, they do seem to retain something of a shoal habit and will remain in a tight grouping for several days or even weeks, before they begin to go their separate ways. It is not uncommon for the fishmongering type of angler, having located such a shoal, to cast into it as many times as is necessary to achieve a bag limit. Perhaps it might take even twelve casts before eight fish are landed. These are indeed still rather silly trout, and there is no way that their capture has anything to do with sport.

In the smaller fisheries, put-and-take principles are usually adopted, and re-stocking may take place every day, in order that stock density remains constant. Usually this involves the transfer of relatively few fish, and it is normal for only one, or perhaps two fish to be put in at any given point. I have been investigating the results of following this practice, with the assistance of several fishery owners, and there is no doubt in my mind that the bulk of fish introduced on any specific day are not caught on that day, or indeed on the following day. In point of fact, there is independent verification of this from a research programme undertaken in America, which showed conclusively over a period of years, that so-called 'wild' trout were far easier to catch than recently introduced trout, and I am convinced that the published facts and figures are quite indisputable.

But what of the question of fighting ability? Does a 15-pound trout fight five times as hard as a 3-pound trout? That is a very difficult question to answer, something akin to asking whether Primo Carnera punched twice as hard as Jimmy Wilde. The bigger the trout, the faster it seems able to swim, and the mass of the fish obviously affects the time and energy taken to stop it. Looking just at the specific case of trout, this means that it is a lot more difficult to stop a big trout doing something than it is to stop a small trout doing the same thing. Under certain circumstances I would use the same fly, the same tackle, to catch a 3-pounder as I would to catch a trout five times as heavy, but the two separate happenings are not at all related. Using a 3-pound leader, it might take as long as two minutes to land the smaller trout, but the larger one might take five times as long, or even – and it has happened – twenty-five times as long. This proves nothing either way, and it is not particularly important. All that you need to know is that big trout fight very hard indeed, and I have yet to catch one that has not fought well enough to tire me more than a little. Anyone who suggests otherwise has yet to hook a big well-conditioned rainbow trout possessing the appropriate number of sound fins.

3 General comment on flies

I suppose there must be literally thousands of different patterns of artificial flies available to anglers nowadays; traditional dry flies, traditional wet flies, 'revolutionary' patterns of either, nymphs, bugs, and lures. It is a great pity that so many of these are quite useless, and would not succeed in fooling a trout even if they could stand up to more than two false casts without disintegrating into their component parts.

Hooks

If one examines these component parts, starting with the hook, it has to be conceded that hooks are not what they were. Points are blunt, barbs cut too large, and the variety of tempers exhibited by individual hooks is as wide as the variety of human tempers obtainable from a random sample of commuters in the London rush hour. In this year of grace, we are capable of sending highly complex machinery into space, of transmitting high-quality colour television from one end of the world to another, but we seem to have lost the knack of making hooks which are consistently well-tempered and sharp.

Dressings

The materials used for actually dressing the fly often leave much to be desired, and it seems to be standard practice to take a carefully devised pattern, and to simplify both the construction and materials used, until the end product no longer resembles the original. Usually this means that the power of that fly to attract trout is radically diminished.

It is the theory of Richard Walker, arguably the best of

present-day innovators in fly dressings, that the trout defines the creatures that it prefers to eat by specific recognition points, which may appear quite minor in relation to the overall shape, size and colour. As an illustration of what he means, he cites the example of someone being sent out on to the streets to find a Chinaman. He may find that everyone he encounters is wearing a morning suit, or a tee shirt and jeans, or an orange, green and magenta striped cloak with a body stocking underneath, but it will not stop him seizing the first Chinaman that he meets, because he has a mental picture of the recognition points enabling him to make his selection, and he will not be put off by non-essentials. So it is with the trout, says Walker; in theory at least it ought to be possible to determine the points that trout recognize, and incorporate these in exaggerated form in a specific dressing which then should be more attractive to the trout.

I see no reason to doubt the basic truth of this theory, and from this one can develop the concept that it may well be positively disadvantageous to change, or simplify, a particular dressing which has proved its attractiveness to trout in its original form.

There are many examples of patterns being offered for sale which bear no relation to the original tyings. Take that well-known lure, Mrs Palmer. The original dressing has a pale yellow goat hair wing that extends well beyond the bend of the hook, a slim white-wool body with silver rib and a turn or two of arc chrome d.f. wool just behind the wing roots, a throat hackle of white cock-hackle fibres, a jungle-cock (or substitute) cheek, and a black head. The pattern in front of me at this moment, which appears to be standard output from at least one source, has a very stiff vivid yellow hair wing cut off square at the bend of the hook, a fat body of what appears to be chenille which is ribbed so tightly that the ribbing material is invisible; there is no throat hackle, and no jungle cock or substitute cheek. And this is sold as a Mrs Palmer. The point of the matter is this: it can be quite disastrous to read that a particular pattern is too good to be without, and yet when you buy that pattern from a dealer you cannot catch a trout on it, because the recognition points have been left out, the mobility negated. Then, quite unjustly, you declare that old suchabody's pattern is worse than useless, although old suchabody is doing very nicely thank you with the original pattern, and pulling out a lot more than his share of trout with it.

If you want to be sure that the dressings you are using are really the correct ones, all you have to do is compare yours with the original tying. That is not very difficult, because a great many books on the subject of fly-tying have been published, and some of them are very good indeed. You can, by making the reference, compare shape, size, colour – everything that you need to establish essential accuracy.

It can also be amusing to browse through old fly-tying instruction books which are now out of print, or which have been published in America. You will be surprised at the number of 'new' patterns which have been 'invented' by somebody over the last ten years, but which are listed under quite another name in these books which may date back fifty years or more. Perhaps it is a case of great minds thinking alike, and then again, perhaps it is not. Who can tell?

If you want to be quite sure that your patterns are correct, and that your tyings are properly durable, then you have little option but to take up the gentle art of 'rolling your own'. I know that many anglers who would like to try, are rather put off by the seeming complexity of the task, and perhaps the sheer finickiness of the operation.

Well, I have large hands, rather clumsy, endowed with a number of stiff, knobbly joints, and usually besprinkled with cuts, abrasions and callouses. I am no expert, far from it, but I am fully capable of tying any of the dressings listed later on, and far more complex patterns as well. I have taught the basic principles of fly-dressing to several people in about an hour or so, and they have progressed beyond the basics very satisfactorily by practice, and reference to books where they cannot quite figure out how something ought to be done. All of these people now tie much better flies than I do, because they practise more. I have a very serious and insuperable problem when it comes to finding time for fly-tying, in that there are only twelve hours in my day whereas there are twenty-four hours in everyone else's. Very odd, that. Should you suffer this same shortage of available time, then find yourself a friend who can not only tie flies for himself, but can manage a few for you as well.

If this proves impossible, then I dare say that you will be able to select the majority of standard patterns from your local tackle-dealer's array, if you exercise some care in the final choice, but you will still have trouble obtaining one or two of the patterns I describe, because they are not popular with the professionals. The main problem is that some dressings are time-consuming, and time is, of course, expensive. No one really believes that an angler will buy a special nymph for 50p, no matter how well it is tied. This may be so, because anglers *en masse* are notoriously reluctant to pay a fair price for their needs, although they seem quite happy to pay grossly inflated prices for non-essentials which may be temporarily 'in fashion'. The truth is that 50p is a fair price to pay for a 'special' such as the Mayfly Nymph, and, until anglers and dealers realize this, the only way that the non-tyer is going to lay hands on them is by stealing them from a friend's fly-wallet, or writing off to one of the specialist fly-dressers who advertise in the angling press. The former technique is not to be recommended unless you are larger than your friend, and better versed in the martial arts, or faster over the ground.

Basic procedures

If you do tie your own flies, there is no doubt that you have the opportunity to create very durable dressings, by adopting certain basic procedures not normally outlined in books on the subject. In all the dressings I list subsequently, it will be taken for granted that these procedures are being followed, and detailing them now will save the constant repetition otherwise unavoidable.

It is usual to start the tying operation by taking the tying silk from some point on the hook shank and running it by close turns to another point where body materials are tied in, after which it is taken back close to the eye of the hook. If these turns are touching, then in effect the hook shank has now received an underbody. Before spinning on the body materials, this underbody should be given a generous coat of quick-drying cellulose varnish (nail varnish perhaps) or Vycoat, which is then allowed to become tacky. The body materials will now be anchored firmly to the underbody, which is itself anchored to the hook shank, and the whole thing becomes much more resistant to wear and tear, and the lacerating effects of the teeth of the trout. There is another advantage too, in that the varnish will effectively prevent iron stain from the hook shank penetrating and discolouring white or light-coloured body materials, and spoiling an otherwise serviceable fly.

The same practice can be followed where feather fibres are spun on to form a thorax, and this offers a considerable advantage where the fibres are brittle, as is often the case with peacock herl. Largish nymphs often require weight to be added under the body materials to assist in efficient sinking, and it used to be standard practice to use copper wire for this purpose. With the very large patterns, this used to result in large bulges above and below the hook shank. It is far more efficient to use lead foil for this purpose, and to add it in the form of strips to the back of the hook shank, so that there is no screening of hook point, and the nymph itself is retrieved through the water with the point uppermost, diminishing the risk of snagging weeds and other obstructions. Suitable foil for the purpose can readily be obtained from wine bottles, although it seems to be regrettable modern practice amongst some wine shippers to use much thinner grades of foil, or even plastic. I regard that as a dreadful practice, quite detrimental to the interests of anglers, and I take care not to buy such reprehensible products.

Assuming that you can obtain a suitable grade of foil, or are alternatively prepared to spend time in beating out lengths of lead wire to suitable thickness, it is very important that it is applied correctly as otherwise you will find that it slips down the shank, taking the body of the fly with it, and collects in a useless and unsightly lump around the bend of the hook. There is often little point in applying just one or two lead strips, when the objective is to achieve a fast-sinking imitation, and the actual amount of lead required may need to be established by experimentation. However, whether the need is for three strips or seven, the principle remains the same.

Cut your first strip to whatever length is indicated by the size of hook, and to a width roughly equivalent to two-thirds of the circumference of the shank, and then bend it so that it will lay nicely along the shank when required to do so. Take several turns of tying silk along the shank, coat this with quick-drying varnish, lay the lead strip on top of this, and fasten it down securely with the silk. Cut the next lead strip a little shorter than the first, and a little wider, apply another coat of varnish on top of the first strip, lay the second on it and secure in the same way as before. Continue in this fashion until you have used the required number of strips, remembering that each successive strip has to be shorter and wider than its predecessor, and that the varnish should not be stinted. Finally, cover the whole thing with tying silk and apply yet another varnish coat before forming the body. This will give you a very well-balanced dressing, which will prove exceptionally durable. Is it any wonder that you could be asked to pay 50p for a dressing that requires this sort of preparatory work before the tying proper can commence? Oh, and do check your hook for temper before you start. There is nothing more infuriating than to near the end of a time-consuming dressing and then break the hook off short in the vice, just because you forgot to test it. So put the bare hook in the vice and give it a good tweak with a pair of pliers before you go any further.

Storing flies

Having gone to a great deal of time and trouble to amass a decent collection of flies, it would be a very great pity if they were kept in such fashion that they were subject to deterioration, and yet this seems to be quite common practice. Meaning no disrespect to the manufacturers of fly boxes in which flies are retained by metal clips, I really think of nothing less well suited to the task of keeping hook and dressing in good condition. The clips themselves are very variable in elasticity, so that one either breaks off points and barbs in an effort to withdraw the chosen fly, or alternatively the flies just slip out, and tangle themselves up with their more firmly secured brethren, or fall out when the box is opened. For some reason, hooks seem much more prone to rust in these boxes too. Then there are the sort of boxes comprising numerous small compartments in which flies are stored. I prefer to regard them as numerous small compartments from which flies may be sprinkled on the ground, usually in conditions of high wind. Similar experiences may be obtained by the use of magnetic strips to retain flies within a box, and I am led to suppose that hooks now contain a very high proportion of non-austenitic metals, which may account for their shortcomings in other directions. Perhaps the ferrous content has been reduced, and replaced by some other metal like aluminium. That would explain much!

I now seem to have drifted into using two different types of container for my flies. The first is a wooden box, fairly large in size, lined with Ethafoam (which does not absorb water) and which holds quite extraordinary numbers of flies. This acts as a basic reservoir from which I can draw off replacements as I need them to replenish the wallets which fit neatly into my pocket. I think that the fly-wallet is a very useful item, and those currently made and marketed by Bob Church seem to be the best of them all. I do wish that they had Ethafoam inserts in place of the standard plastic foam, but that is a minor quibble.

Flotants

Flies which are intended to float should float, and over the years some quite remarkable substances have been diverted to that end, although they may originally have been intended for some other purpose. Boracic ointment was one favourite, as I recall, and I possess in my collection of oddities, a tin of Red Deer Fat from Hardy Bros which is described as being 'for rod joints &c.' but which was used for the anointment of dry flies by many anglers who secretly believed that the flavour thus imparted rendered their fly almost irresistible to the trout. Who is to say that they were wrong? Even after all these years, that tin of deer fat has a penetrating odour, and in its day, it must have been quite overpowering.

Fortunately, in this day and age, we do not have to rely upon products such as these, because the finest of all flotant materials is readily available. I refer of course to Permaflote, which is perhaps the only truly efficient flotant ever devised. A correctly dressed dry fly soaked in Permaflote can even float again without more attention after a trout has been caught on it, and I doubt that higher recommendation is possible.

It is scarcely necessary to worry about products designed to assist a nymph to sink quickly, because when this is needed, a pattern carrying a suitable amount of lead can be used, and for a slow sinker, it is rare to need to do more than spit on it to ensure that it is sufficiently waterlogged at the time of the first cast. This is perfectly efficient, if perhaps slightly lacking in dignity.

4 Nymphs and bugs

My observations over the years have led me to the inescapable conclusion that trout feed mainly sub-surface, and that the floating fly is, for much of the time, just a little icing on the cake. I imagine that this will be regarded as an infamous suggestion by some of the die-hard purists who appear never to have learned anything about trout in all the years that they may have been fishing for them. Why, I have even heard it said that the nymph-fisher should be banned because he teaches trout to grub for food at the bottom. An elaboration of this theme is that because too many small trout are taken sub-surface and returned as undersized, they develop an unwillingness to approach the surface again, and hence prove impossible to induce to rise to a floating fly. Have you ever heard such nonsense?

Examination of the stomach contents of brown and rainbow trout from a wide variety of waters, some rarely if ever fished, shows that almost anything is acceptable in the dietary habits of trout. Snails, worms, shrimps, larvae, pupae, bread, terrestrial insects, tadpoles, frogs, leeches, fag ends, bottle tops, daphnia, small fish of all species: all is grist to the mill. The so-called 'cannibal' trout almost always turns out to be a poor old specimen nearing the end of his life cycle, and probably incapable of even finding food. If you care for the term 'cannibal', then correctly apply it to all trout, of whatever size and whatever species, because cannibalism starts at the fry stage, with the smaller, sicklier specimens being eaten by their larger, healthier brethren; in the case of brown trout, it continues until they are too old and feeble to hunt live food, and manage to subsist for a while on carrion.

Rainbows are ferocious devourers of fry, and I have taken a fish of less than a pound in weight which contained no fewer than fifteen tiny roach fry. On the other hand, the bigger the rainbow

gets, the less that small fry seem to figure in their diet, and I have
yet to find any at all in the stomach contents of 10-pound-plus
trout. I think that the important factor is the leisurely mode of life
of the big rainbow in still water, to which I have already referred. I
am not suggesting that they never eat small fry, but I do believe
that for most of the time, it is just too much trouble for them to go
chasing after evasive little creatures, although they may well con-
sume dying or dead ones if they happen to come across them.

The reasoning angler will rapidly come to the conclusion that,
for the greatest chance of success, he should probably rely mainly
upon the sunk fly. The question is, what fly? There are so many
different patterns available, that it would seem almost impossible
to own more than a tiny fraction of them. This is where the necessity for careful observation pays dividends, and it will very soon
become apparent that the range of traditional wet flies is worse
than useless. No matter how prolonged the sub-surface scrutiny, at
no time will the Butcher, Bloody Butcher, Peter Ross or Blue Zulu
be seen – let alone Colonel Downman's Fancy! So it is probably
quite safe to disregard this type of pattern, and concentrate more
upon imitations which do at least bear some resemblance to
natural forms of life. This narrows the field considerably, and it can
be narrowed still further – in my experience, at least. A fairly
limited range of nymphs and bugs proves adequate for my purposes, and since these are all fairly simple patterns, even the most
amateur of fly dressers should be able to produce more than
enough to meet his needs.

Midge pupa

It is a rare still-water fishery that does not contain a population of
midge pupa, although you may more commonly hear these referred to as 'buzzers', 'buzzer pupae' or, fairly infrequently, as
chironomid pupae. This is the intermediate stage between the larval form, known to everyone as the bloodworm, and the adult
midge. It comes in a variety of sizes and colours, and is probably
one of the easiest of patterns for the amateur fly-dresser to
attempt. The tying silk is taken to a point about one-third of the
way round the bend of the hook, which should be fairly fine in the
wire. A fine strand of floss silk is tied in, plus a length of ribbing
material, which can be white hackle stalk, white tying silk, or fine

silver wire. A bunch of about a dozen white cock-hackle fibres is laid along the back of the hook shank, projecting beyond both bend and eye, and the tying silk is taken back over these, securing them firmly, to the point where the thorax commences. The floss is now wound back to the same point, forming a slim body, which is then ribbed on the opposing spiral, tied off and the waste ends of floss and ribbing cut away. Three or four strands of feather fibre, often peacock herl, are now tied in, twisted into a 'rope', and wound on to form the thorax. This is tied in, and a whip finish formed just behind the eye, and underneath the white hackle fibres. These fibres, which represent breathing tubes, are now clipped short.

Midge pupae are found in a very wide variety of colours, and sizes, but I have found the most consistently useful colours to be black, scarlet and orange. Black pupae should be tied in sizes 8, 10, 14 and 16; scarlet in sizes 14 and 16; orange in sizes 16 and 18. The exact shade of orange is important, and is described as 'hot orange'. There is no harm in extending the range of colours if you wish, and you can include yellow, green, brown, grey and olive, and these can most usefully be tied to sizes 12 and 14.

There are some minor variations to this basic pattern, which may be effective when standard patterns are not. There is a variant on the black pattern which, on its day, can be very killing. This has a wide gold rib, and a slim thorax constructed of the same floss as the body. You merely spin the floss on up to the eye, bringing the ribbing up and tie it off, take the floss down again about one-third of the way, take it back to the eye, and finish off as usual. The thorax should not form a hump, but should have sides parallel to the hook shank.

Another variant on the black midge pupa theme has a couple of turns of red feather fibre at the junction of body and thorax. An orange pupa variant, best tied on sizes 12 and 14, has a wide gold rib allowing only a very narrow band of the orange body material to show between the turns of ribbing, and the thorax should be of hot orange feather fibre.

Yet another variant, which may not be a pupa imitation at all, but is tied by exactly the same technique, except that the breathing tubes are omitted, has a body of white floss silk, a slim white or very pale feather-fibre thorax, and a tag of scarlet, hot orange or green. Rib colour is not important, and I use a length of fine monofilament.

Turning on the nymph

There is no need to impart any action at all when offering the midge pupa to an observed trout, which will usually be seen taking the natural no more than three feet deep, and usually much closer to the surface film than that. The leader is greased to ensure that the imitation is suspended at the correct depth in the path of a feeding trout, and only if it is necessary to realign it need it be moved. Obviously, it is desirable to offer an imitation as close as possible in size and colour to that upon which the trout is feeding, but if your offering is inspected and refused it is necessary to try an alternative. For example, a trout which is eating very large black pupae and which ignores a perfect imitation frequently will accept a tiny hot orange pattern. When a much smaller black natural is the chosen diet, the gold-ribbed narrow-thorax version will often pay dividends as the change fly. If all else fails, one or other of the white variants may prove effective. Under normal circumstances it is not necessary to ring these changes, but it is as well to be prepared.

Freshwater shrimp

Established fisheries usually have a freshwater shrimp population, and at times trout can become preoccupied with feeding upon them. It is not at all an uncommon sight to see a big trout lurking close to a weed-bed, picking off the shrimps which every now and again dart out into the open water; or even browsing over minor algal growths or clear gravel, sucking in shrimps by the dozen. At such times, it is rare that anything but a shrimp imitation will be accepted, and in order that it is accepted without too much demur, the colour ought to be a reasonable match. Shrimp colour tends to vary from water to water, and the observant angler will have taken careful colour note before tying up his imitation. The simplest way to investigate such matters as colour, and indeed average size, is to pull out a mass of weed from the water, shake it over a piece of plastic sheeting, and then transfer all life forms obtained in this way to a jar of water. Not only will specimens of shrimp be obtained, but many nymphal forms also. In this way, very accurate colour copies can be achieved.

Size is of lesser importance, but I believe that a case can be made out for offering an imitation slightly larger than the run-of-the-mill naturals.

There is advantage in adding lead to this dressing, and three or four strips of lead foil should be tied to the back of the hook shank. The body is of wool, and the colour shade depends upon the colour of the shrimp in the particular fishery, as I have already commented. If you assume that the average colour is a sort of olive, then you can vary this to your specific requirements by mixing in a small amount of different colours to achieve a lighter or darker appearance. For example, Richard Walker recommends a mix of green, fawn and pink, which creates an odd pinkish-olive which is very effective on some waters. Where the natural is very dark, the pink should be omitted and replaced by chestnut, or similar shade. Yellow can be used in place of pink, where a paler shrimp is needed.

Wind on the body material over the lead strips, using brown tying silk, and then on the opposing spiral, add a body hackle which is preferably large buff cock – unless you have specific local knowledge to indicate an alternative colour. Using sharp scissors, clip the back and sides very close, leaving bunches of fibres projecting down to imitate legs. Apply several coats of varnish to the back, until a reasonable imitation of the shell is achieved. I have experimented with a strip of polythene tied in to simulate the shell, but it is rather susceptible to the wear and tear induced by trouty teeth, and varnish makes a much more durable finish.

If the trout that you are stalking is a lurker at a weed-bed, try to cast your shrimp so that it sinks slowly between trout and weeds. An overcast can be remedied by tweaking the shrimp back rather jerkily, and this can be a useful gambit at those times when the trout does not take on the drop. A fairly lightly leaded dressing is most useful in this situation. Where you are fishing to a bottom browser, use a more heavily leaded dressing, and cast in such a way that you can retrieve very slowly, in tiny twitches, across the path of the fish. Hook sizes for this pattern can vary between size 10 and size 14, but I would tend to restrict usage of the larger hook size to the pursuit of the bottom browsers, when it is often advantageous to have a quick-sinking dressing slightly larger than usual.

Water beetle and the Green Beast

Some years ago I devised a dressing intended to represent the larval form of one of our larger water beetles, and achieved considerable success with it in a wide range of waters. It was christened the 'Green Beast', and as such it has been known ever since. It now has a number of colour variants, so I suppose these should be known, *in toto*, as the 'family of Beasts'.

The tying is simple. Using a round bend, wide gape hook, and dark green tying silk, tie in a few grass green hackle fibres to form a short tail, silver wire for ribbing, and a length of grass-green floss silk. With the floss, create a fat, carrot-shaped body, and rib on the opposing spiral with the silver wire. Prepare a speckled partridge hackle, long in the fibre, by cutting off all fibres on one side of the stalk, tie this in, and take no more than two turns of it, before tying off. With the tying silk, build up a small head, and whip finish. That is the basic Green Beast, tied to sizes 10 and 12, and all the other Beasts are tied in exactly the same way, in scarlet, grey, brown, black and orange. The only variant from this pattern has the grass-green body with a rib of hot orange d.r.f. silk.

Water beetle larvae pursue a rather erratic jerky course through the water, presumably as they pounce upon something edible, and then pause to eat it. This indicates the method of fishing the artificial, and indeed the occasional tweak which moves the fly no more than two inches, followed by a long pause, seems to be consistently effective. A medium-speed continuous retrieve seems to make this pattern attractive to smaller trout, although what they take it for I cannot imagine.

I tried tying the Green Beast in larger sizes, as large as a long shank 8, and incorporating lead foil into the dressing, and although the occasional trout succumbed to its charms, the majority did not, indicating that something was wrong with the basic pattern when expanded to larger size, and none of the alternative colours was any better.

Damselfly Nymph

Then I encountered a dressing of the Damselfly Nymph. Strictly speaking, I suppose this looks more like a Dragonfly Nymph, because the latter is fairly heavy in the body, while the former is very slim. Nevertheless, it is a very effective pattern and has accounted for a good many big rainbows. In appearance it is similar to my big Beast pattern, has a fat carrot-shaped green body, a short green tail, and a speckled partridge hackle, very sparse. The difference appears to be in the body material, which in this case is made of very well-mixed blue, green, yellow and orange wool, giving an overall impression of lightish green. This, when wet, does not change significantly in shade, whereas the floss silk body darkens appreciably. I do not know why this colour change is acceptable when the dressing is on a size 10 or smaller, but unacceptable on a size 8 long shank, but there it is.

The Damselfly Nymph is quite deadly early and late in the season, but I personally have not done too well with it mid-season, which again I find inexplicable, as indeed I find many things in angling.

This is an excellent pattern for fishing to trout lying deep, particularly when dressed with six or seven strips of lead foil on the back of the hook shank. Being heavy, it quickly sinks deep, works very well hook point upwards, and is easily kept under the closest observation. The long, sparse hackle fibres impart a strong impression of life, and it appears to offer the trout a very satisfying mouthful to chomp.

Heavy dressings such as this do cause casting problems, and when one first tries, it happens all too frequently that it drops down on the back cast and, if by chance it fails to tangle in long grass, it will certainly come through so low on the forward cast that it will either hit, or wrap itself round the rod. That is preferable to it smacking one in the back of the neck, which also happens, and this can be positively injurious! If people ever wonder why I wear a deerstalker cap, tilted rather far back, now it can be told. I wear that hat, in that way, to protect the back of my neck from fast-moving, heavily leaded nymphs on size 8 long-shank hooks.

Mayfly Nymph

One of Richard Walker's patterns and an absolute must in any fly collection is the Mayfly Nymph, also correctly dressed on a size 8 long shank, and carrying anything up to seven strips of lead foil on the back of the shank. He has amended body material at least twice since he first devised the dressing, and I for one think it would be very difficult to improve on the latest recipe.

Tie in the required number of lead strips, and cover the whole with brown tying silk. At the start of the bend, tie in a half a dozen cock-pheasant-tail fibres with the tips forming short tails; a strand of Angora wool, very pale buff in colour; and a length of brown tying silk for ribbing. Wind on one turn of the wool, followed by one turn of the butts of the pheasant-tail fibres. Then another turn of wool, another turn of the fibres, and then complete the abdomen with the wool, ribbing with the brown silk, tying in, and finally cutting off the loose end of the ribbing. Take a large bunch of pheasant-tail fibres and tie these in with the points projecting far enough beyond the eye so that they may, in due course, be brought back to form legs. Continue to wind wool forward to form the thorax, which should not be any bulkier than necessitated by the lead strips. Pull the pheasant-tail fibre points back, to form the legs, and secure these in place with a figure of eight binding. Bring the butt ends forward over the thorax, and tie in. Cut off all waste materials, and build up a sleek head with the tying silk before making the whip finish. Take a dubbing needle and pick out tufts of wool on each side of the body between the turns of ribbing. Trim these to even length with sharp scissors, and a suitable length is equivalent to about half the width of the abdomen. Varnish the head, and at the same time apply a narrow streak of varnish along the back of the abdomen and thorax, being careful to avoid getting varnish on the legs and tail. The careful man will apply three such coats.

Not very often will you see this dressing offered for sale in a tackle shop, and if you did, it would probably cost two to three times as much as the average lure. The reason for this is quite simple. I have already instructed how lead foil strips should be applied, and this is obviously time-consuming. The tying itself is quite straightforward, but the subsequent varnish applications also take extra time.

This is yet another difficult-to-cast pattern, until you get the hang of it, but is admirable for the deep-lying fish, and is particularly attractive when the induced-take technique is employed, by allowing it to drop slightly below the level of the trout, and then lifting it up, slowly and smoothly. Sometimes it will be taken on the drop, sometimes the trout will wait a few seconds and then follow down and pick it delicately off the bottom, and sometimes it will make a determined lunge on the vertical retrieve. A sideways movement past the trout's nose can be effective, but less so than the retrieval systems mentioned first. Prospecting the gravel banks can pay off in the very early days of the season, but rarely for longer than that.

There is one problem with this fly, and that is the fact that it can be used too much, and the trout become very frightened of it. For example, great publicity was given to the superb catches made on it during the early part of the 1977 season, with the result that every angler visiting big-fish waters made sure that he was armed with copies, which ranged from excellent to diabolical. Very few knew how it should be fished, and the tendency was to fish it rather fast. Sometimes once came to rest in front of a whopper, which took it, and after a short struggle broke free – never to succumb to that imitation again!

In fact, although a good number of anglers hook big trout on the Mayfly Nymph, it seems that relatively few actually succeed in landing such fish. Fortunately, it is quite easy for a trout to rid itself of a bulky dressing on a long-shank hook, so no serious effects would be noted, except the tendency for any such trout to rush off in haste when offered another copy of the dreaded thing that stung them when they tried to eat it.

Some anglers discovered that they could only catch the smaller trout, say around the 3- to 5- pound mark, when they followed the fast-retrieval syndrome, and were quite content to continue to pick off a regular supply of fish of this size, so it has become quite a familiar sight to see the Mayfly Nymph fished lure-fashion. That also tends to put the big fish off.

Apart from the above-mentioned dressings, which are all attempts to imitate very closely a natural life form, there are several 'utilitarian' patterns which can be very killing, and which bear a vague resemblance to a number of different life forms.

Chomper

A very useful pattern is the Chomper which bears family likeness to shrimps, hoglouse, and even sedge pupae. It is a simple dressing to tie. Take the tying silk close to the bend and tie in about four strands of ostrich herl, and a length of Raffene. Twist the herls into a loose rope, spiral them up to the eye and tie off. Stretch the Raffene, which should previously have been dampened, over the back, tie in at the eye, cut off all waste and finish with a neat head. Varnish the head, but not the Raffene. I have found size 12 to be the most generally successful, and have rarely succeeded with larger or smaller sizes. Suitable colours are: white herl and brown back; amber herl and brown back; olive herl and brown back; amber herl and buff back; green herl and buff back; hot orange herl and buff back. Retrieve can be the usual slow, jerky twitch, or the attempt made to take fish on the drop.

Pheasant Tail Nymph

Arthur Cove's Pheasant Tail Nymph can be a real killer on its day, and a very simple tying it is, too. Tails, body, wing-cases are all of cock-pheasant-tail fibres, and the ball-shaped thorax is usually made of wool. I have enjoyed most success with a buff thorax, but other colours can be very effective, and I would rate white, black, scarlet, olive and hot orange as being very useful on occasion. I am convinced that it is best to fish this nymph static, or virtually so, and where deep water has to be negotiated, a few strips of lead foil firmly anchored under the thorax will overcome buoyancy problems. Hooks should be long shank, fine in the wire, and can range from size 16 up to as large as you like. Where there are rules on a fishery restricting the size of dressing, this is a very suitable pattern for tying short. If that sounds puzzling, let me assure you that there are one or two fisheries where the rules say that the fly itself, from head to tail tip, must not exceed one inch. Well, this would be about the size of a PT Nymph tied on a size 14, or maybe a size 12. Believe it or not, you can transfer that size of dressing to a long-shank 8, so that it looks a bit like a low-water salmon fly after a severe attack of mange, and it will still catch trout.

Grizzly Beetle

The Grizzly Beetle is a pattern that not many people have encountered, and yet it can be used to convey an impression of many different life forms. The dressing is quite easy. Use a size 10 wide-gape, round-bend hook, quite heavy in the wire, and using black tying silk, fasten in at the bend three black ostrich herls, a black, white and grey cock hackle, fairly long and stiff in the fibre and a bunch of seven to ten cock-pheasant-tail fibres. When tying in the hackle, allow half a dozen or more fibres to project backwards to form a longish tail. Take the tying silk back to the eye, twist the ostrich herls into a loose rope, and spiral up to the eye to form an underbody. Tie these off, removing waste, and then wind the hackle, palmer-fashion, on the opposing spiral, tying off and removing waste. Bring the pheasant-tail fibres up over the back, tie off and remove waste. Finish with a neat black head, which should be well varnished.

Fish this pattern to suit the occasion. I have used it dry, well proofed with Permaflote, to imitate horseflies or houseflies which had somehow found their way in considerable numbers on to the surface of the water. It has proved successful when the trout were shrimping, or taking corixae, and refused the most perfect imitations, and I have taken fish with it when they did not appear to be feeding at all, and refused almost everything else thrown at them. It has one disadvantage, and that is poor hooking ability, possibly because the long stiff hackle fibres impede the hook point. Clipping the fibres appears to lessen the attraction to trout, and the only solution I can offer is that of a much harder strike, which necessarily entails the use of a more powerful leader.

Plastazote Corixa

Trout eat a lot of corixae, and corixa patterns abound, but I seem to have little success with any of the standard tyings. I have caught a few on Dave Collyer's fine dressing – the Plastazote Corixa – which is so buoyant as to be unsinkable, but is intended to be fished on a sunk line. Since I can find no place for sunk lines in my big-trout hunting, the only times that I dare use the dressing is when fishery rules do not explicitly forbid the addition of a split shot to the leader. The technique is very simple. Establish the depth at which a trout is feeding – or, rather, how far off the bottom it is feeding. Pinch a lead shot on the leader at about the same distance from the corixa pattern, and cast to the area where feeding is taking place. The shot sinks to the bottom, while the corixa remains anchored to it, suspended at what you hope is the right depth. If the trout takes it at all, it will be with absolute confidence, but sticking the hook in requires a rather longer sweep of the rod than usual, because you have to pick up a lot of loose leader.

Having mentioned the technique, I shall decline to provide the exact dressing of the Plastazote Corixa, because it may be that if you use this style on a small still-water fishery which does ban the use of shot on the leader, I could be blamed by the fishery owner for leading you astray. That would never do.

I would not be without two patterns which I believe are attributable to Tom Ivens, namely the Black and Peacock Spider, and the Brown and Green Nymph. Goodness knows what trout take these patterns for, but take them they do, and I would not be without them.

Black and Peacock Spider

First, the Black and Peacock Spider. With black tying silk, tie in at the bend of the hook a length of black silk floss and four strands or so of peacock herl. Take the silk back to the eye, and spiral the floss on as an underbody, which should be slim at the tail end but fairly thick at the thorax; tie off and cut away waste. Twist the herls into a rope and wind on in the opposite spiral, tying off and cutting away waste. Tie in at the head a largish black hen-hackle fibre, and take two turns only before tying off and making the whip finish. This fly should be fished either very slowly, or static, at virtually any depth. There seems little advantage in adding lead to the dressing, and where a deeply sunk version is needed, this is best dressed on a heavy wire hook. Size of hook can vary from as large as you like, to as small as you can be bothered with, but I suppose I tend to use a size 12 hook more than any other. I do tie variants to the basic pattern, of which the most successful has a red floss underbody which just 'grins' through the peacock herl when the fly is wet. Provided that care is taken in the tying, and the underbody well-varnished, this is a very durable pattern.

As an example of this durability, on the last day of the 1975 season I was fishing Avington and had managed to catch one very fine rainbow of some 12 pounds on a Black and Peacock Spider variant. I think this had a red underbody, and a greyish-black hackle. Later on, I lost it up a tree – one of my failings – and after trying several other patterns without success, switched to a standard B and P Spider dressed on rather an oddly shaped hook. Quite late on in the day, not having seen another large trout move in the bottom or middle lakes, I returned to the top lake and eventually found the largest trout I had ever seen in the fishery up to that time lurking in a corner. I hurriedly stripped off line from the reel, and tried a speculative cast which, by a fluke, landed exactly right and was promptly taken. This was one of the fast-running brigade, and it set off for the other end of the lake at a greater speed than I had ever experienced previously. Unfortunately, a loop of line had slid round my reel, and by the time I realized this, the tension was so great that I could not free it, and a badly placed bush prevented my running along the bank to relieve the pressure. Of course, the leader parted, but that is possibly not the end of the story.

On the first day of the 1976 season, Richard Walker hooked a trout within ten yards of the spot where I had hooked and lost that fish; after he had landed it, the weight was officially recorded 18¼ pounds. Firmly embedded in its cheek, he found the tatty remains of a B and P Spider, minus hackle, and yet with enough body left to identify it correctly. In conversation with Walker a few days later, the subject of this fly came up. He did not know of my little catastrophe, and I did not know that he had found a fly already in the cheek of his trout, until I mentioned my loss. He then told me of his finding, and without his giving me any clues whatsoever, I identified the fly and even provided a description of the hook – which fitted.

Of course, this is not incontrovertible proof, but it would seem to be a *prima facie* case, specially since no other person on the fishery with Walker that day admitted losing a fly, let alone a B and P Spider, in a trout before the time that the big one had been landed. This says much for the durability of a decently tied fly, and also serves to illustrate that some of the Avington monsters most definitely are residuals.

It is interesting that I estimated the weight of the trout that I lost as about 16 pounds or so, roughly 1½ pounds heavier than the record at that time, caught by Julian Farmer, yet Walker's trout was about 2 pounds heavier than my estimate. I do not believe that I could be as far wrong as 2 pounds, having seen my fish very clearly, so the implication is that the excess weight was made up in the intervening period, when natural food is rather scarce, and low-water temperatures slow growth to a marked degree.

Brown and Green Nymph

After that digression, let me return to the matter of the dressing of the Brown and Green Nymph. Take brown tying silk to the bend of the hook, and tie in first of all four strands of peacock herl with the tips projecting backwards to form a tail. Then tie in two strands of ostrich herl, one dyed leaf green, and the other dyed brown, and a length of oval gold tinsel. Wind the ostrich herls so as to form a body which has alternate segments of green and brown, rib with the tinsel, tie off and remove waste. Bring the peacock herls forward over the back, tie down securely, and then twist the remaining lengths of herl into a rope, and spin on three turns to form a big head. Tie off and whip finish after removing waste. Tom Ivens used this pattern fished fast, and considered that trout took it for a stickleback. What it looks like to a trout, I have no idea, but I do not fish it fast because no self-respecting big trout would look at it if I did. I use this dressing fairly exclusively when I can see a big trout moving around in a hole in the weeds, but cannot induce it to accept anything else. I suspect that it may be taken for one or other of the more common nymphs. Following the standard practice of too many anglers, I ought to change the ribbing from oval to flat gold tinsel, use a different herl for the body, and re-christen it the Last Resort, because that is exactly what it is. I object to a pattern that I cannot identify as imitating a natural food item; I rather resent it that the trout should know more than I do, but there it is.

Green Partridge

At those times when clumps of green algae disengage from the lake bed, and float up to the surface, and before prevailing winds assist these chunks to form a solid mat, big rainbows may often be seen cruising the vicinity at depths from six inches to a foot, feeding upon something that the naked human eye cannot identify at any distance. In fact, the food item is a tiny green worm – almost certainly the larval form of a species of chironomid. At such times the Green Partridge is invariably a killing pattern.

The dressing is simplicity itself. Take a long-shank size 8 hook, and spin on a slim body of lime-green d.f. wool (according to my suppliers, the correct colour nomenclature is phosphor yellow!). The length of the body should not exceed one inch, which leaves a lot of bare shank showing, but this does not matter in the least. Add a sparse speckled partridge hackle, and finish off in the usual way.

This dressing is so balanced that it will commence to sink at exactly the correct rate as soon as it hits the water, and provided that the cast is accurate, is rarely refused by the trout.

I do not think that anyone really needs a wider selection of nymphs and bugs than the few listed here, but I dare say that I will have changed my mind by this time next year. That is one of the enchanting things about angling; that nothing is fixed and immutable, everything is subject to change. May it always be so.

5 Dry flies

I used to think that everyone knew the difference between fishing the dry fly, and fishing the wet fly, but now I am not quite so sure. Several times in recent seasons I have met gentlemen fishing traditional wet flies and even lures, in the firm belief that they were indeed fishing 'dry fly' because they only had one fly on the leader, were using a floating line and not one of those beastly sinking shooting heads, and were adamant they were not using a bally weighted nymph. Do you find that difficult to believe? I assure you that it is perfectly true. I would stress that only some of the gentlemen in question were British, which may soften the blow slightly. When you consider that this abysmal ignorance is prevalent throughout angling, it is hardly any wonder that 80 per cent of trout are caught by 20 per cent of the anglers. Some authorities put it as high as 10 per cent of anglers catching 90 per cent of the trout, but the truth probably lies between the two.

Just in case there should be even the remotest doubt in anyone's mind, a dry fly sits on the surface film – floats, if you prefer. Oddly enough, it is fairly rare for big rainbows to display much interest in floating flies, but every now and again the unexpected occurs. Almost invariably, the fly in question is a large one, and usually has to be present in sufficient numbers for it even to be worth tying on an imitation.

I suspect that the real truth is that big trout take far more floating flies than is suspected, but this is probably related to permitted fishing hours on most of the small still-water fisheries that contain whoppers. Normal start time is 9 a.m., by which time it is almost certain that any morning surface activity is over. Closing is usually either 9 p.m. or dusk, whichever is earlier, but in either case it is too early as a rule for an evening rise to develop. Even if one is permitted fair latitude in determining dusk, it has usually become too dark to be able to determine whether a rising trout is large, small, or indifferent, and I have yet to satisfy myself that the splashiness or otherwise of an actual rise has very much to do with the size of the trout that is rising. This may be different elsewhere, but on the fisheries that I visit most regularly, you cannot be sure of the size of the trout taking a floating fly at dusk unless you succeed in hooking it.

Accept the fact that dry-fly fishing for big trout is merely a minor gambit, and you will not go far wrong, but I do not mean to imply that you should not be suitably armed to cope with the situation if it arises. Perhaps you need no more than two basic dressings, although one of these is capable of several permutations of size and colour.

Sedges

Without any doubt at all, those flies which we know as Sedges have tremendous trout appeal, and the most important is the Great Red Sedge. At the risk of seeming repetitive, I have yet to find a better dressing than that devised by Walker, and which may be tied to a size 8 or 10 long shank hook, round bend, and fairly fine in the wire. Take brown tying silk to the hook bend and tie in a tag of one turn of arc chrome d.r.f. wool, then three strands of chestnut ostrich herl. Take the tying silk back up the shank, twist the herls into a rope, wind these on to form a body, then tie off. With very sharp scissors, trim the herl as close as possible to the body, to achieve a velvety texture. The wing is a goodish bunch of natural cock hackle fibres cut square level with the bend and waste trimmed off close to the eye before tying in two really good, stiff, natural red cock hackles. Before use, soak well in Permaflote.

This dressing is fished either static over a rising fish, or alternatively cast well beyond that fish and drawn back at great speed into the area, so that a definite wake similar to that created by the natural insect is induced. The take may come while the fly is moving, or it may not come until it is static, and in either case it is quite certain that you will be taken by surprise!

Another useful dressing is created in exactly the same way as the Red Sedge, but using pale buff materials on a long-shank 12 or 14. I really do not think it worth bothering with any of the other

Savage rise to the Red Sedge

members of the sedge family, because if these two dressings fail, then so, probably will any of the alternative colours and sizes.

The same style of dressing can be used to imitate that big white moth that sometimes appears at dusk, flounders on the water for a while, and usually ends up being engulfed by a hungry trout. This can be tied on a size 6 or 8 long-shank, round-bend, fine-wire hook. The body is cream ostrich herl, and is best tied rather fat over an underbody of white floss silk, and not clipped close like the sedge patterns. The wing is a big bunch of white feather fibres allowed to project beyond the bend before being cut square. Two hackles should be used, and these may both be top quality white cock, or as a variant, one white and one buff hackle. Fishing technique is more or less the same as for the sedges, but the pulls across the surface should not be as long.

Crane Fly

When the Crane Fly or Daddy Longlegs appears in great numbers, trout usually take a distinct liking to it, but for some reason most of the artificials that were produced were singularly unsuccessful as deceivers. There is now a very effective dressing available. Use a size 10 long-shank round-bend hook. Take your light brown tying silk to the bend, tie in three or four strands of swan secondary feather fibre dyed a dirty sepia, return the silk to the eye. Twist the feather fibres into a rope, and wind on to form the body; tie off and cut away waste. Take half a dozen pheasant-tail fibres and tie two knots in each (not the easiest of jobs!) to form the legs which should be tied so that they trail backwards. This is essential; any other position for the legs renders the tying quite ineffective. Tie in two cree cock hackle points, forming backward-slanting wings, and finish with a long-fibred ginger cock hackle.

This fly has to be fished absolutely static, and a good soaking in Permaflote will ensure floatability.

Fishing dry flies

I am sure that many people fail to hook trout on the dry fly because they simply do not know when, or how to strike. The usual problem is that in the panic-stricken second of an unexpected take, there is an automatic reflex strike administered by the excited angler, resulting in the fly being pulled out of the trout's still open mouth. There really is no need to hurry, and usually all that it is necessary to do is wait until the line begins to move away as the trout swims off with the fly in its mouth. This is the time to pull the hook firmly home in as relaxed a manner as possible, and avoid snatching or jerking.

If anyone is disappointed that I have not provided a greater variety of dry flies, I can only excuse myself by saying that I have taken only a very small fraction of my large trout by this means, and therefore I do not regard it as a particularly successful technique. Those who prefer to fish the dry fly, and intend to stick to their preferences at all costs, are very welcome to do so, and I will commiserate with them right now on the basis of my forecast of their lack of consistent success. I do not regard any form of fishing with an artificial fly as being more or less sporting than any other form; it is just that adherence to an inefficient mode for the task in hand is scarcely conducive to the desired results being achieved.

6 Lures

Think of fishing a lure, and the picture immediately springs to mind of ranks of anglers busily double-hauling away, and hurling lures into the middle distance; then dragging them back through the water just as fast as they can manage without the aid of sophisticated machinery. Were we, as a race, to be blessed with fast-flowing, crystal-clear rivers, fed by melting snows, and carrying large stocks of migratory and/or non-migratory rainbows of truly exceptional size, then it might be that such tactics would prove unbeatable.

Instead, we are faced with the problem of very territorial rainbows dwelling in what are mainly small still-water fisheries, and which have settled for a much more casual way of life. Long-casting and lure-stripping, even where permitted, is a singularly inappropriate way of attempting to catch these big rainbows, and that apart, it is not really very much fun anyway.

Nevertheless, there are times when one can use certain types of lure successfully, where fishery rules permit their use, and there are times when they will produce results obtainable by no other method. When the water on a fishery is particularly murky, and this may be attributable to mud stain or high density of suspended algal forms, a lure can mean the difference between a blank day and a red-letter day. Nothing could be simpler than the recommended method, and there are few more boring ways to fish. You have been warned.

Where to fish a lure

It is a very great advantage to know your fishery, to know some of the normal feeding areas, but if you do not know it that well, and cannot obtain local advice (which is usually not worth having, unless you know the donor very well), then the difficulties are exacerbated. Since you cannot see very far into discoloured water, you cannot tell what lies beneath the surface, and normal ambush tactics are therefore out of the question. If there is an inflow into the fishery of water that is less murky than the lake itself, then this makes a goodish starting point for the exercise, but if no such feeder stream exists, then perhaps it may be of assistance to use a leaded fly, and in this rather inefficient way, plumb the depths around a spot that smells productive. If you cannot 'smell out' productive areas, then you will have to select a place that looks as if fish ought to be there, by reason of wind direction, or bank-side growth, or some indicator of like nature.

Perhaps I ought to comment on the suggestion that one can smell potentially productive areas. Smell, is of course, not at all the right word to describe an intuitive feeling, a sort of sixth sense, but frequently the presence of fish seems to be conveyed through the nose. That fine angler Fred Taylor most certainly can 'smell' fish, and I have noticed that a great many children also seem to possess the ability to sense the presence of fish in one swim as opposed to another, even though they might be too young to put their conviction, and the reason for it, into words. As a child, I most certainly possessed the ability, but I do believe that it tends to diminish in most of us with the passing years. I have pretty well lost the facility now as far as most species of fish are concerned, but every now and again I find that I am aware of the presence of a biggish trout before I have actually seen it. I can remember, dimly, that carp and tench possess quite different 'odours', and big rainbow trout 'smell' different from either. To me, small rainbows and brown trout are quite 'odourless', but the more that I study brook trout, the more convinced I am that they too have their own particular brand of 'odour'. If that sounds too mystical for your scientific mind, I am sorry, but nothing will make me retract a word of it, because I am not putting forward a wild theory. I know! And there are those who have experienced something similar and will understand.

By whatever means available, an area to fish will have been selected. If the water is very deep, too deep for bottom to be reached on even the longest leader, then a sinking line will be obligatory, unless you possess that contraption designed to hamper efficient casting, the sink tip line. The purpose of the exercise is to fish the static lure, in the hope that it will be picked up by a foraging trout. Surprisingly often it is, and sometimes the obliging trout proves to be quite exceptional for the fishery.

You cast out, allow the lure to sink to the bottom, and then wait patiently. If you are in luck – and luck is an essential part of this method – then the take will be signalled by a tightening of the line, and your part in the exercise is to continue the tightening until the hook is pulled home. Actually, it is quite rare to miss on the strike. However, should much time pass without event, then draw the lure towards you, perhaps a foot, perhaps two feet, but no more than that. Then wait patiently again.

Choosing a lure

I said it was boring, and so it is, but it can put good fish in your bag while other anglers remain fishless. Much depends upon the choice of lure, though, and I believe that any lure fished in this way, in such conditions, should contain a high proportion of white in the dressing.

I suppose the best of the predominantly white lures is the Jack Frost, but the Baby Doll will also prove effective. Basically, the actual tying pattern is relatively unimportant, and you might as well invent your own static pattern if you decide that you wish to fish in this manner. I believe that bulk is important, so a fattish body of white wool or ostrich herl is a good start point. To this you can add a white cock hackle tied palmer-fashion over the body, and perhaps some strands of marabou tied in over the back. Under some conditions a touch of red seems to be beneficial, so you could add a throat hackle or tail of scarlet feather fibres, or include some scarlet strands in the white marabou. Bulk and visibility is the sole objective in the tying of a static fly, plus the fact that it ought to look worth eating.

Improvisation

Just once in a life-time, something may happen that you will never forget, and which serves as an object lesson in the need to be able to improvise. I can recall one such occasion, while fishing the Shiya river in Ethiopia. I had been working very hard to induce a take from a gang of very big rainbows that I had located in a large, deep pool just below some rapids, but they were all totally uninterested in anything I offered. Then, out of nowhere appeared an immense number of large, gaudy dragonflies, which performed their mating rituals in the time-honoured way, and occasionally landed on the water; by accident or design I never established. Every time such a landing occurred, there was a swirl, and a 'cloop', and the dragonfly vanished. I tried the largest dry-fly patterns in my wallet, but even the biggest Mayfly dressings were ignored. Finally, in desperation, I found some lures that were roughly the right sort of colour and size, and after treating these liberally with Permaflote, cast one out to see what would happen. Even with the Permaflote treatment, the lures were, to say the least, terribly inefficient floaters, but that did not seem to matter too much, because they did not get time to sink. Within a second of their alighting on the water, they vanished in a very satisfying sort of way, and I found myself connected to a series of really powerful trout, some of which I actually landed. To my great surprise, most of these were brown trout in the 5- to 6-pound class, and I had been totally unaware of the presence of anything other than big rainbows in that pool. Perhaps it was that I had concentrated my attention on the rainbows, because of their sheer bulk, but had ignored the smaller browns. Sometimes one sees only what one wants to see.

From the foregoing, you may have gained the impression that I consider normal lure-stripping to have no place in the armoury of the pursuer of big trout, and you would be absolutely correct. However, one never knows when one needs a 'wild card' up one's sleeve, and I would not dream of setting off on a fishing trip unless I was fully equipped in the fly department – which, in my terms, means that in addition to nymphs, bugs and dry flies, I also have a box of lures. They may not ever be needed, but you never know.

7 Leaders

It may seem odd to commence a dissertation on tackle by opening with the subject of artificial flies, and then moving on to leaders without a mention yet of rods, reels and lines. To me, this sequence seems perfectly logical, because the trout dictates the size (and pattern) of fly that will be used; the fly size dictates the leader strength because one cannot achieve correct presentation when the leader is too heavy, and breakage risks are too high when the hook is too large for the leader. The strength of the leader pretty well dictates the power and action of the rod if the tackle is to be balanced correctly; the line size is dictated by both the rating of the rod and the distance that has to be cast. The reel is there solely by necessity!

Leaders now are almost invariably of nylon monofilament, although I do have some gut-substitute leaders tucked away in their original envelopes that I may pluck up courage to use one of these days – just for fun, I hasten to add, and then only after exhaustive testing. The old 'x' ratings are still given to leader material, although it is quite meaningless nowadays, but fortunately some manufacturers provide a plethora of alternative statistics, including diameters and breaking strains in good basic English (plus metric equivalents for those interested).

Because nylon monofilament varies in quality, it is not really adequate to talk in terms of diameters, and for that reason alone I shall adhere to breaking strain in pounds weight, and assume that most sensible people will know what I am talking about.

Leader size

The selection of a leader to suit a particular fly size is really very simple. Hook sizes 18 and 16 usually will accept a leader of 3- to

4-pounds breaking strain. Frankly, it would be desirable to use a lighter gauge to achieve a better presentation, but bearing the potential size of hooked trout in mind, one dare not take the risk. Hook sizes 14 and 12 are well suited to a leader of 4- to 6-pounds breaking strain, although one could reduce to 3-pound stuff with the size 14 in very clear water conditions. Hook sizes 10 and 8 are well catered for by 6- to 8-pound leaders, but the size 8 hook should always be restricted to the 8-pound leader unless it is very fine in the wire, and exceptionally sharp. Few are.

There is my conveniently short list of leader sizes associated with hook sizes, and it is my firm belief that adoption of this concept will allow excellent fly presentation, allied with great hooking power.

Leader construction

I must say that the general construction of leaders has caused me much concern. I am sure that everyone has read and noted the instructions propounded by many excellent fly fishermen on the assembly of leaders from lengths of monofilament of varying breaking strains, in order to achieve a nicely tapered effect, and which turns over and lays down well on the water. All very scientific and well reasoned, but I hate these knotty pieces of nylon! Every knot is a potential risk point for breakage, as well as possessing tremendous powers of attraction for bits of floating rubbish.

I suppose it has the advantage of cheapness, but this is greatly outweighed by the risk factor. I refuse to take avoidable risks that can make the difference between a fish on the bank, and a fish left to swim around with a hook in its mouth, trailing a knotty length of nylon behind it. These days it is possible to purchase highly efficient ready-made leaders which taper smoothly from butt to tip, and thus only require one knot apart from that securing the fly. Of course, manufacturers spoil their image by making them with a great loop at the butt end.

My preferred leader assembly is simple. First of all, to the tip end of my fly line, I needle-knot about a yard of 18-pound monofilament, and apply several coats of Vycoat to the junction of line and leader to achieve the joint requirements of smoothness and sealing. This extension piece remains in being until it is too short to be of further use, at which point I cut off the knot and tie in a new extension. This obviates the necessity to make an inefficient and

Author with 17¾ pound rainbow trout

Figure 1   Needle Knot

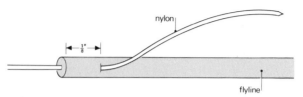

a. Perforate fly line with pin. Point end of nylon and thread through

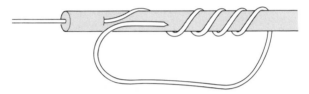

b. Wind nylon round fly line, bring end back and lay alongside

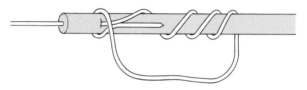

c. Take turn of nylon back over itself

d. Wind over until the original turns are used up

e. Pull hard on ends of nylon, then on nylon where it enters fly line. Cut off loose end, varnish over all

obstructive knot between line and a leader loop every time the leader is changed. Why not use one of those new plastic gadgets for joining line and leader? Apart from the fact that I do not trust them, they also have the disadvantage of not passing through the rod rings without major risk of jamming, which proves something of a problem when using a very long leader and trying to net a big trout!

Figure 2   Single Grinner Knot
Shown with three turns – four turns increases strength by about 4%

Having previously cut off the loop at the butt of the one piece tapered leader, I now Grinner-knot it to the extension. This knot is formed at the point of maximum diameter of the leader, and on the brand that I use most regularly, this appears to be identical with the diameter of the 18-pound extension; hence this makes for a very efficient knot. For safety's sake, I usually apply a couple of coats of quick-drying cellulose varnish to this grinner knot; an easy task if you are prepared to steal a bottle of your lady's nail varnish. Well, you could hardly go into a shop and buy it, could you?

I always use a Grinner knot to secure fly to leader, and feel that there is great advantage in applying varnish to this knot too.

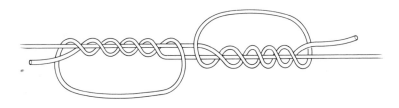

Figure 3   Double Grinner Knot
Shown with three turns each side – four turns increases strength by about 4%

I do not care for the appearance of ready-made leaders (or indeed for the appearance of monofilament in general), because they have too much glitter about them, and before I set off fishing, I always make sure that I have an adequate supply of pre-treated leaders. The leader is given a prolonged bath in silver nitrate and then treated in a bath of photographic developer; this turns the leader a rich reddish-brown colour and removes much of the flash as well.

It is suggested that this treatment can lengthen the life of monofilament because it protects against the weakening effect of ultra violet radiation. I have no opinion on that score; my leaders never last more than one day anyway, because I cut them off at the end of a session even if I have already made several changes during the day.

I also use Dylon dyes on my leaders, without noticeable ill-effects. Some are dyed brown, some are green, some are olive, but more often than not they are dyed a variety of shades. This is achieved by coiling them loosely, and dipping just a section of the coil into a prepared dye bath. When the desired shade is attained, the process is repeated by transferring an undyed part of the coil to another dye bath of different colour.

Whether I am too pedantic, I do not know, but my reasons for following this procedure are detailed in the chapter dealing with lines. All I can say is that I do succeed in catching big trout where very many others fail, and this may be due in part to the care I take in ensuring that my leaders are as non-reflective in appearance, and as mechanically efficient as I can make them.

For the past season, I have been experimenting with level leaders, and although I have restricted myself to the heavier gauges of nylon, I am not too dissatisfied with results so far. The main problem is that it is necessary to reduce the strength of the extension to the reel line, as otherwise the grinner knot becomes inefficient. So I reduce the strength of the extension to 10-pound monofilament, and in theory at least, knot a length of 8-pound stuff to this. In practice, I have made at least one mistake that could have had serious consequences, by using a length of nylon with breaking strain of around 2 pounds lower than the 8-pound nylon that I thought I was using. Obviously I was lucky not to have paid the penalty for such incompetence.

I am not too happy about this leader system, I must confess, because the knot strength at these lower breaking strains is obviously the weak link in the system. Mind you, the 10-pound extension has its own advantage for fishing the static attractor fly in mucky water, as described in the chapter on lures. In this case, one can forget all about tapered leaders, and long leaders for that matter, and just tie the fly on to the one yard extension piece. This may seem extraordinarily short, but it is perfectly effective.

Leader length

That leads to the question of the optimum length of a leader. Well, I fish in some very clear waters indeed, and have rarely felt the need for a leader of longer than four yards. Since the ready-made leaders are usually three yards long, and the extension piece is a yard, then I automatically have my four yarder, unless the extension is nearing the end of its working life, in which case I would sooner switch to another line with a longer extension than knot in a supplementary length between butt of leader and extension. The alternative is to needle-knot in a new extension after cutting off the old. This can easily be accomplished as a bank-side job, but it just wastes valuable fishing time.

There are times when a shorter leader than four yards can be advantageous, specially when fishing very close to the bank, and this is very easy to set up. All I do is tie in a leader of lower breaking strain that I actually require, and chop off as much of the business end as is necessary to reach the desired gauge. What could be easier than that? As I recall, Hardy Bros used to market a leader with instructions detailing how much to cut off the business end in order to achieve certain tip strengths. This was an excellent idea. Unfortunately, the butt end included a length of heavy nylon suitable for needle-knotting to the line as the extension, and this seemed to be rather gilding the lily as well as inflating the price.

Droppers

My failure to mention droppers may cause surprise, particularly in those who have missed the implications of everything I have said so far. I do not like droppers and do not use them because they have no place in big-trout fishing. At best, a dropper will be ignored by the trout, and at worst it will contribute to its loss when hooked. I referred in an earlier chapter to losing a very big rain-

bow at Grafham. The story is this. I was boat-fishing with Jack
Ludkin, a fairly frequent companion of mine in those days, and
attempting to find a decent trout or two by offering on the point a
leaded Green Beast with orange rib and, as a dropper, the standard version of the same fly with the silver rib. I hooked into a
trout which was obviously bigger than anything I had contacted at
Grafham before, and a very long, hard fight ensued. I experienced
the greatest difficulty in getting this trout up off the bottom,
because I could not get it under control at all, but eventually it
made up its own mind to come up, and it surfaced at Jack's end of
the boat, and wallowed there for a while. I could only see the
commotion, not the trout, and I yelled at Jack to try to net it if he
could without risk. He picked up the net, which was not a small
one by any means, and then just froze. I shouted again, but his
reply was to shake his head in amazement, and insist that the net
was too small! Then the trout sounded again, and the line ran
vertically down from the rod, but there seemed to be very little
activity. I took a chance and peered over the edge of the boat. The
water was clear, and I could just make out my leader with the
dropper fly jigging slightly, and below that I could dimly see an
immense rainbow shaking its head slowly from side to side. Before
I could take any further action, a much smaller rainbow came
zooming through the water and smashed into the dropper. There
were some almighty thumps and jerks, and the leader came back to
me, broken at the dropper. Since that day I have never used more
than one fly at a time, and my catch rate does not appear to have
suffered as a result.

I should make one further point on my attitude to leaders. Before I
start fishing I test the needle knot, and the double and single
grinner knot, looking for a weakness that might result in a lost
trout. After every cast, I check each and every knot again, without
fail. After I have landed a trout, I cut off the fly, test the hook
again, and retie it to the leader which is then subject to another
severe testing. I have deliberately forced myself into this procedure, until it is now second nature and I regard it as a standard
preliminary to each cast. Whether you decide to follow the same
practice is very much up to you, but it has much to recommend it.

Exhausted author nets another huge rainbow

8 Rods

I have always expressed the view that in any particular branch of angling, there is ample scope for personal preferences in the selection of tackle. The only stipulation I would make is that, when very large trout are the quarry, personal preferences should not be allowed to over-ride the efficiency of correct tackle balance. Without this balance, the playing of a big trout becomes a hazardous business, even more hazardous than needs be, and risk factors are quite high enough already without increasing them still further by an adherence to unsuitable rods.

It is probably true, or at least manufacturers believe it to be true, that the majority of trout fishermen are reservoir anglers. It is hardly surprising, therefore, that by far the greater majority of fly rods offered for sale have this usage in mind. A reservoir fly rod is a very carefully engineered instrument, and in the case of glass-reinforced plastic, more generally known as hollow glass-fibre rods, this nowadays requires adherence to certain basic design principles. The walls are ultra-thin, for lightness, and this has to be associated with wide diameters, tapering abruptly towards the tip, creating a rod in which most of the action is restricted to the tip. In order to cast a long line with ease, line speed through the air has to be maximized, and this is ensured by creating very fast tip action. Of course, the double-haul cast assists in increasing line speed, and this particular style of casting also requires much of the rod's length to be rather stiff, in order that the power necessary to generate speed is not dissipated by non-essential flexing.

This type of rod is usually excellent, when put to the purpose for which it is designed, but with the possible exception of one rod, is quite inappropriate for the specific tasks of casting short distances with accuracy, and playing big trout on relatively fine leaders.

I think no one would disagree that most reservoir stock fish are pretty small, and yet the angler tends to use heavy leaders and largish lures, partly because this has become the standard, and partly because too many leader breakages are suffered when breaking strains are reduced to a lower level. Try to use a powerful reservoir rod for big trout, particularly when a smallish fly is obligatory, and you will find that you are unable to exert a necessary level of strain on that trout, because the action of the rod is such that there is no shock-absorbing capacity. What happens is that the trout begins to play the angler, which is quite the opposite of what should be happening.

A perfect example of this occurred early this season. I visited Church Hill Farm Fishery in company with Ray Riley. Ray is a very well-known Buckinghamshire match angler, who has also, in the last four or five years, become an enthusiastic trout angler, usually fishing the reservoirs. He has, because of his match-fishing background, considerable experience in playing fish on what seems to me to be ridiculously light tackle, and perhaps because of this he tends to use a leader which is really too light for his rod although he suffers few breakages. On the day in question, he was tackled up with an AFTM 9 reservoir rod, and a level 4-pound leader. About mid-morning he hooked a trout which he had on for a while before I joined him to see what was going on. He told me that the fish was gigantic, and when it actually came up and broke surface, I was forced to agree. My estimate put it somewhere around the 15-pound mark. With due respect to Ray's skills, that trout did exactly as it pleased with him, because at no time was he able to carry the fight to the trout, and pressure it as it should have been pressured. It was the classic case of the fish playing the angler. Some thirty minutes passed, and the trout was still as strong as ever, although Ray was flagging slightly. I felt that the writing was on the wall though, and at last the inevitable happened, and the hook fell out.

There was nothing wrong with the strength of the leader in relation to hook size and water clarity. The fault lay in the rod itself, which was possessed of such extreme tip action that in the particular sequence of events it was of about as much assistance as a poker would have been. Had Ray increased the pressure on that trout to the extent necessary to control and tire it, the leader would have broken at the first sudden pull. Since big trout are always lunging unexpectedly, or shaking their heads violently, and since this specimen was no exception to the rule, the leader would have

Church Hill Farm Trout Fishery

been broken very early on in the fight. The lack of proper pressure on the fish not only meant that it was allowed to do exactly as it pleased, but also contributed to a major extent to the hook-hold loosening. The longer this one-sided struggle continued, the more certain it was that either the hook would fall out, or that some weakness of the leader would have developed to the point of failure. Riley is an intelligent angler, and realized the problem very early on. It would have been better if he had realized it before

tackling up, because there was always the chance that he would hook into the trout of a life-time. He will never make that mistake again.

Choosing a glass-fibre rod

If you consider the various aspects of the problem – big, strong trout, smallish fly, relatively fine leader – it becomes apparent that the rod has to be able to provide a cushioning effect to the leader. It also has to be taken into account that you do not need an efficient long-casting rod. What you are left with is a requirement for a rod capable of bending throughout its length, and possessing a certain capacity for power transmission which I find very convenient to relate to an AFTM rating. As a guide, this may be thought to be rather rough and ready, but I find that it works admirably in practice, provided that one is not too heavily reliant upon the rating given by the manufacturer, which may be inaccurate, and is prepared to undertake some simple testing oneself.

For a good many years, I used just two rods for big trout, both from the ABU Feralite range. The smaller rod was 8½ feet in length, a very soft supple rod; although the AFTM rating was given as No. 7, in my judgement it was undoubtedly a No. 6, and was overpowered by a No. 7 line for anything other than very short casting. This rod handles, very efficiently, leaders in the 3- to 5-pound class, and enables considerable leverage to be applied without risk of leader breakage. I use a simple test procedure, which is to tackle up, embed the hook in a convenient tree trunk or branch, stand some fifteen yards off, and begin to exert strain with the rod held high to ensure maximum curvature. With this small rod, it is just possible to induce breakage at the tip with the 3-pound leader, but almost impossible to break the 4-pound leader, just as long as the rod is kept well up. Obviously, I cannot induce breakage of the 5-pound leader. So this rod is adequate for the correct presentation of fly sizes 18, 16, 14 and even 12, on the correct leader, provided care is exercised.

The other ABU rod is a 9-footer, having a rating of AFTM 8–9, but more correctly rated at No. 8. This is again a slim, supple rod, with the action running full length, and by the crude testing technique indicated earlier, I found it possible to break a 5-pound tip, but almost impossible to induce breakage at 6 pounds, with no risk at all at 7 or 8 pounds. This proved ideal for leaders in the 6- to 8-pound class, enabling correct presentation of the larger dressings on sizes 12, 10, 8 and even No. 6. Usage of this latter size is pretty well confined to the presentation of the dry White Moth.

These assemblies appeared to meet my requirements of tackle balance admirably, and provided that I maintained my fetishistic checking of leader prior to each cast, I was able to fish in the sure and certain knowledge that if I was broken, it would be entirely due to my incompetence, to a mishandling of a situation, and no blame could be vested in my tackle. Indeed, I was broken just twice by big trout in the three seasons from 1974 through to 1976, and one of these breakages is referred to in the chapter on Nymphs and Bugs. The other was a similar example of ham-fisted negligence, in that I allowed a particularly heavy trout to build up to a tremendous speed on a long run, and then clamped down on it far too abruptly, with the result that the leader broke at the knot. I was, in point of fact, using the 3-pound leader on the smaller rod, but I think that the result would have been the same had I used heavier nylon. Instead of applying gentle braking, I locked the line solid against the cork grip with my fingers; the inertia of the trout moving at that speed, pulled the rod over until it was pointing down the line, and before I could slacken off, and return the rod to the vertical position, the breakage had occurred.

I do not mean to imply that playing a big trout on this tackle was all sweetness and light; far from it! Although I was able to maintain good pressure on the trout, I was not always able to circumvent their worst machinations, and even though the rod was bent into a hoop for most of the playing time, it still seemed to take an inordinate while actually to bring the trout to the net. On one occasion I recall, the trout was pretty well played out but was still wallowing just out of reach of the net, and I was restricted in my own movements by the steepness of slope of the bank, and a large bush to each side of me. Since I could not get nearer to the trout, it obviously had to come nearer to me, and I increased pressure by taking the rod butt back behind my head, at full stretch of my arm. Retrieving line was not possible at that stage, because my left hand was fully occupied by the landing net, and since the trout was finally moving towards me, I did not want to sacrifice my advantage by dropping the net and recovering line. The trout continued to come, but I noticed a strange tapping noise very close to my right ear. I risked a quick glance, and found to my horror that the tip ring was rattling on the reel. Imagine the shape of that rod! Fortunately, the trout surrendered at that very moment, and I was able to net it without further complication.

I tried another rod with a very high reputation, the Richard Walker Superlite by Hardy Bros, and found this to be a delightful weapon, although it needs to be teamed with nothing less than 8-pound leaders if the safety margin of tackle balance is not to be dissipated. This is rated at AFTM 7–8, but seems to be a very much stiffer rod than my pair of ABUs. In practice, it works well,

Application of maximum strain to bring a trout to net

but does not seem to kill trout any more quickly than either of the softer rods, and I had become resigned to the necessity of taking anything up to fifty minutes to kill a big trout. It seemed far too much time to spend, and presented problems apart from tackle strain that devolved upon my physical condition.

First of all, let me say that when I pull a hook into a trout, I turn my wrist over as I draw line with my left hand, and once I am assured of a firm hook-hold, I glance at the watch now clearly visible on my wrist. As I complete the final netting, I again check my watch, and the period of time that has elapsed between hooking and netting is known to the nearest minute. So there is no guesswork in my timing at all, not like the man who plays a fish for three minutes and firmly believes that it has been at least an hour.

My problem is that after I have been maintaining full pressure on the rod with my right hand for ten minutes or so, I first develop 'pins and needles', which is rapidly followed by numbness and total loss of sensory perception. At this point, I am obliged to switch the rod to my left hand, clamping the line against the cork grip, and do nothing but keep the pressure on while I shake my right hand furiously to restore sensation. Fortunately, this does not take very long, and I am then able to transfer the rod back again, and once more carry the fight to the trout. Within ten minutes I have to repeat the procedure, for exactly the same reasons. In the course of a battle raging for fifty minutes, I may have to resort to this crude physiotherapy some half a dozen times, which is inconvenient to say the least.

Then it occurred to me that the problem of these overlong battles might possibly be connected with the very nature of fibre-glass rods. Even my easy actioned rods have a relatively wide circular cross-section, and while this particular section is very resistant to bending, there is the tendency for it to become slightly oval as bending occurs. Oval sections are far less resistant to bending than circular, and so a progressive increase in ovality occurs, which means in simple terms that the more the rod bends, the softer it becomes, and the amount of leverage applied to the trout is diminished significantly. This provides an excellent safety margin I suppose, but it did seem to imply that the more power I exerted, the softer the rod became, and that maybe I was having to step up my own power output in a totally uneconomic way.

Choosing a carbon-fibre rod

At the end of the 1976 season, I began to experiment with carbon-fibre blanks, which have a much narrower diameter than their hollow glass counterparts. I found that a wide variety of actions are available, and I eventually selected a number of blanks as being worthy of further investigation. It seemed to me that carbon fibre, far from becoming softer with increased bending, tended to reveal a cumulative, if minor, stiffening. If this was true, then it seemed that a rod of this material was more suited to my specific purposes than was glass fibre, because at least there would be no diminution of pressure on the trout as I exerted more power

The first fierce run of a big rainbow

to bend the rod, and that leverage would be transmitted more efficiently to the trout.

In practice, this seems to be the case. I have fished now with both types of rod, have caught big trout with both types, and in every case the trout played on a carbon-fibre rod has come to net in a very short time, compared with the norm on a glass-fibre rod. I have not suffered the same physical problems of loss of sensation in my playing arm, which is in itself a great asset, but I seem to achieve the same level of physical exhaustion at the end of the fight, in spite of the shorter time that I have actually been working on the trout. Perhaps this is a psychological thing, rather than a physical.

So now my armoury of rods has been increased, and I possess a quite unnecessary number for the task in hand. Leaders of 6 to 8 pounds are fished on either an 8½ foot, or a 9¼ foot carbon-fibre rod, both with an AFTM rating of 7–8. Leaders of 3 to 5 pounds are fished on either an 8 foot, or 8½ foot carbon-fibre rod, both of AFTM 6 rating. In addition, I am still experimenting with two other rods. One is 8 foot, AFTM 4, and apparently capable of balancing a leader of 2 pounds, this for ultra-clear water conditions, and the tiniest of flies. The other is 10 feet, with a rating of AFTM 6–7, which appears to be efficiently capable of handling any leader from 4 to 8 pounds, and will probably have maximum usage in those waters where obstructions abound, and greater rod length may be necessary to assist in steering the trout away from such danger zones. The problem is that carbon fibre is such a new material to me, that I have not yet been able to ascertain fully its advantages and disadvantages. For the purpose to which I put these rods, no disadvantages have yet become apparent, and only time will reveal whether any exist, other than price. Similarly, I may well not be aware of all the advantages.

I have just obtained a pair of the new ABU fly rods marketed under the trade-name 'Carbolite' These are constructed from a calculated mixture of both glass and carbon fibres, in the ratio of 30 per cent glass, 70 per cent carbon. It is early days yet to offer detailed comment, but my initial impression is that ABU have got their mix right. The rods feel slightly less stiff than pure carbon, which I believe may be advantageous in the shorter lengths, but there appears to be no excess addition to either weight or diameter. Certainly, as far as the smaller sizes of trout are concerned – say 7 to 9 pounds – they handle beautifully and assist in a quick kill. My favourite is the Carbolite 78, which is 9 feet in length and has an AFTM rating 7–8. The element of softness in action indicates that I can safely use leaders 5 to 8 pounds, and practical tests suggest that I could even fish as light as 4 pounds without too much risk. Time will tell! The addition of glass to the construction appears to eliminate the cumulative stiffening in action with bending, but without the reversion to increasing softness as a result of ovality.

You may have noticed that I use the name 'carbon fibre', rather than 'graphite' because I do prefer to give things their right name. When I am catching trout, I would not think it sensible to call them chub, or eels, or carp, although they are all fish too. Carbon is a natural element which can exist in a variety of forms, of which coal, diamonds, soot and graphite are all examples. Everyone knows that soot, although it is pure carbon, is a soft powder, but you might as well say that you have a soot rod, as a graphite rod. Graphite is a finely crystalline form of carbon, used in the manufacture of pencil leads and blacklead for grates, as well as many other things. It is about as possible to make a fly rod out of graphite as it is to make one out of soot. The fibres of carbon used in rod construction are quite dissimilar to graphite, soot, or diamonds, even though all are forms of carbon.

Rod fittings and finish

When it comes to rod fittings, I have no firm opinions to offer. It does not matter to me whether rod rings are snake, or bridge; whether lined or unlined, as long as they are light, neat and unobtrusive. I tend to regard the new single-leg rings as a potential snag hazard, but this may be more founded in prejudice than reason. I do like cork grips, because they feel pleasant to the hand and are lightweight, but I have used composition grips without being conscious of any disadvantage. All that I demand from a reel fitting is that it shall be not too heavy, not too flashy, but most of all that it shall be efficient. There is nothing more exasperating than a reel which keeps dropping off while you are playing a fish, and I do not much care for the sort of fitting that becomes so enamoured of the reel that it declines to release it when required to do so.

One thing I am quite adamant about, and that is that the rod shall have a non-reflective finish. Some manufacturers will persist in ruining an otherwise excellent rod by dressing it up with gold or silver foil, lurid whippings, highly polished reel fittings, and scintillating varnish, so that it bears an unholy resemblance to Christmas decorations in a Buenos Aires brothel. The amount of reflection from such rods is quite remarkable, and they give off brilliant flashes of light when the sun catches them. I can think of only one thing more likely to frighten big trout, and that is referred to in the chapter on lines. It is essential that the flash is removed from your rods, and nothing could be simpler than applying two or three coats of matt varnish. It can make the difference between failure and success. Why go to the trouble of advertising your presence to the trout?

I do like a 'light' rod. This is very vague terminology, and conveys very little unless expanded slightly. I find that a built cane rod is too heavy for me, and I do not feel comfortable with one in my hand. Hollow glass-fibre can be very light, and I am perfectly happy with rods of this material. Carbon-fibre rods can be lighter

Bob Church under pressure from a 15½ pound rainbow

still, which to me is yet another benefit. On the other hand, a certain rod is, of course, no better than another, just because it is ⅛ ounce lighter. Try arming it with a reel and line weighing 10 or 12 ounces and see how much difference you can notice!

Within limits you can indulge your preference in the choice of rods for big trout. It is a mistake to think that you need a big powerful rod, and if you bear in mind the necessity to achieve the correct balance between leader strength and rod action and power, it does not really matter whether you opt for built cane, hollow glass fibre, or carbon fibre. You always have options regarding length, and the most important deciding factor here is that it can be very difficult making short, accurate casts with a long rod.

Never be content just to assume that you have balanced your tackle correctly; go and test the balance by sticking your hook into a tree and pulling for a break. Test, check and re-check. Leave no room for error, because big trout never give you a second chance.

9 Lines

White or coloured line?

Some years back, a number of cine films were taken of me fly-fishing in Africa, and a great many colour slides too. Clarity and colour quality were excellent, but there seemed to be considerable variation in the visibility of the fly line. In some cases it was virtually invisible, but in others it was so clear that it seemed to glow brilliantly like a neon sign. Eventually the mystery was solved, and the brilliantly sparkling line was revealed to be one of the new white lines that someone had given me before my tour commenced, and which I had quite automatically loaded on to a reel, without giving the matter a second thought.

We all experience good days, and bad days, because that is the nature of fishing, but the more I thought about this white line, the more obvious it became that I was getting more than my fair share of bad days when I used it. Then I forgot all about it again, because I had too much else to think about. Rather later on, back home, a major dispute built up in the correspondence columns of the angling press over the relative merits or demerits of the white line, and this raged on until editors decided that enough was enough, and declared a closure of that argument. Opinions were so widely varied, and so many views were given by so many people, that really the subject did become the most ghastly bore. And yet, it was quite obvious that there was something terribly wrong about the white line, and I could not understand how it ever came into being.

Then I happened by chance to meet the managing director of an international company concerned with the manufacture and marketing of fishing tackle. (He and it shall remain anonymous.) During conversation the claim was made by my MD acquaintance that it was his company that had undertaken all the research and development of white fly lines, and that everyone else had merely jumped on the bandwagon. I had, and have, no great desire to test the veracity of that claim, but naturally I showed considerable interest in the research aspects.

As I understand it, an environment was created whereby fish – presumably trout – could be retained in natural surroundings, but kept under continual observation by the researchers, who were themselves not capable of being observed by the trout, and filmed records were made of reactions of the trout to, amongst other things, fly lines. Apparently these lines were submerged below the surface, and after exhaustive tests had been carried out there appeared to be massive proof that trout were least scared by a white line, but progressively more scared by lines of darker colour, and especially dark green and dark brown lines. Findings were checked and re-checked; there seemed no possibility of error, and so the white fly line was born.

I asked question after question, but my informant adhered exactly to this summary and varied not an iota from it. I was surprised that he did not notice the illogicalities himself, but obviously they just failed to occur to him, perhaps because he was far too close to the situation to be able to take a long, cool look at it.

The first illogicality is patently obvious. The tests were carried out with submerged lines, and yet the eventual production was of floating white lines, not sinkers. It happens to be fact that if you submerge a white body in an environment where the amount of light reflected subsurface is roughly equal to the amount of light penetrating the surface, that white body becomes quite difficult to see. Since the test environment was set up in such a way that filming sub-surface would be easy, it has to be assumed that the water was very clear, and that the bottom was composed of light sand or gravel. The same principle can be noted, say, in the Indian Ocean, where the amount of light reflected from white coral sand is very high, and a submerged white object virtually vanishes. The effect is considerably reduced when reflected light is low in comparison with direct light, as is normally the case in a fishery where there may be some silting up of the bed, and dark patches of weed exist.

Unfortunately, this does not hold good when a line is floating at the surface, because now the main light source is behind the line, when viewed from below, and since the line is opaque, it is seen as a silhouette against the light source. Silhouettes are always black.

No matter what the actual colour of your floating line, whether it is white, orange, yellow, brown or green – or, indeed, black – it will always appear to be black when viewed from below, unless reflected light is greater than direct light. Which is impossible in a natural freshwater environment, or virtually so.

So, what have we discovered so far? Experiments have proved a white line to be less visible than other colours when it is submerged, and on this basis, floating white lines have been produced which are no more, and no less visible than lines of any other colour. That seems quite extraordinary logic, but maybe it ought to be regarded as a harmless gimmick devised to persuade anglers to buy more fly lines, a standard marketing practice in any consumer-orientated production unit.

Unfortunately, there is much more to come. Accept, if you will, the over-simplification that a colour is created because of an ability to absorb and reflect light, and that white is white because it reflects light very efficiently. This is why houses in the tropics tend to be white-painted, and tropical garb is also white; because it reflects light most efficiently. (Light at the infra-red end, is also heat, and thus since white reflects all light, coolness is retained.)

So now we have a line, no less visible than any other line when floating, which reflects vastly more light than any other line while it is being aerialized and extended over the water. The principle is not vastly different from retaining the high gloss on a rod, except that the reflections from the line are infinitely more damaging, because it is closer to the fish. On a clear day at Grafham, one can stand at the lodge and see very well the flashing of an aerialized white line nearly a mile away, although rod flash is very unlikely to be seen at the same distance. How any sensible, logical individual can still believe that a white line is beneficial, I simply cannot imagine, and it does underline the need for tackle manufacturers to retain, in an advisory capacity, intelligent *practical* anglers who might be able to prevent them from indulging their wilder excesses based upon research which has been badly conceived and even less well interpreted.

I would like to advise you not to buy white lines, but from examination of tackle dealers' shelves, I realize that it might be almost impossible to obtain an alternative. So buy a white line, but do not use it!

Dylon dyes are quite excellent for changing the colour of fly lines as well as leaders. A wide range of colours is available, and you merely make up a batch of dye at double the strength indicated by the instructions. Some lines will accept dye at 60 °C, and others need a shade higher temperature. There is an element of risk involved if the dye bath is too hot, and the wise man will experiment with a scrap of spare line before risking prolonged immersion which could damage the plastic coating. The required immersion period may be as long as two hours, and the temperature of the dye bath should be maintained if possible. This can be achieved by putting the dye container into a much larger bowl of water at the right temperature, and topping up this larger bowl at regular intervals, with boiling water. Of course, the technically minded will use a small water heater, thermostatically controlled, submerged in the dye bath.

Basically you can dye your white line any colour you wish, because anything will be less reflective than white. You can try black, brown, green, olive, grey – but I prefer to use more than one bath of dye, immersing part of the line in each, to achieve a very mucky looking camouflage effect, mainly in brown and olive, but all streaky and spotty. My reasoning is quite simple. Different colours possess different light reflective properties, so the combination of two or more colours on a line ensures that reflection is variable throughout. I may be wrong about this, but I believe that it has advantages.

Other questions about line

That takes care of line colour, but what of the line itself, the profile, the characteristics? There are so very many different sorts of lines now available. They float, or have neutral density, or sink slowly, or more quickly, or very quickly indeed, or just the tip sinks. There are double tapers, forward tapers, bug tapers, torpedo tapers. Some of them are so incredibly sophisticated that it seems a pity that they cannot fulfil their prime function; that of assisting in the smooth execution of a cast. Frankly, it is almost impossible to cast some lines, which seems something of a paradox.

However, all these mysterious marvels need not concern you, because there is unanimous agreement amongst reasonable anglers that the profile of the double-taper line lends itself admirably to accurate and delicate casting. And, of course you do not need the whole of a double taper line.

Let us assume that you have purchased a floating double-taper line, rated at AFTM 6. It is very unlikely that you will need to cast more than about fifteen yards of this, so why not cut it in half, and convert it to a fifteen-yard single taper? It will cast just as delicately and accurately as if you still had another fifteen yards of it on the reel. But suppose that, because your rod is three yards long, you decide to cut off that much from the butt end of the line. It will still cast as delicately and accurately as before, and yet you will have made a shooting head, which is banned from some fisheries because it 'lands on the water too heavily, causes too much splash, and frightens the trout'. What a lot of nonsense some people do propound!

There are advantages in using half, or a little less, of a double-taper line. First, you may find a friend willing to take the other half off your hands for half the price of the whole line. Second, you can put a half line plus all the backing line you need on to a smaller,

The nitrate-treated leader shows clearly in this take to the Daddy Longlegs

and hence lighter reel than you would need for the whole line plus backing. Third, if a trout sets off on a long run, there is that much less thick fly line for water pressure to react upon and perhaps damage hook-hold.

If you use monofilament backing, and I think that the flattened monofilament has much to recommend it, then you can use that line as a shooting head for reservoir fishing, if you ever indulge in that form of recreation. On the other hand, should you restrict your activities to small fisheries where long casting is neither necessary or desirable, you have the option of normal mono-filament backing, which is cheap and good, or perhaps using fine plaited terylene, which is expensive and good, and takes up even less room on the reel than 20-pound breaking strain mono-filament. In the latter case, one can effect yet a further reduction in reel size and weight. To my mind, the arguments are all in favour of half lines, and now it may be clearer than it was from whence one obtains pieces of scrap line to test the effect of dye bath temperatures on the plastic coating.

The half line is attached to the backing by means of the needle knot, after which the heavy shoulder at the butt end of the line should be very carefully pared down to achieve a taper similar in shape to that of a pencil after it has been sharpened. The junction of line and backing should then be coated with Vycoat, although some people prefer Araldite. The purpose of the exercise is, of course, to streamline the junction so that it passes readily through the rod rings without snagging. Even if you use a full double taper, the principle of backing-line attachment remains the same, except that you will not need to use a sharp instrument to taper the fly line down, because it should already be sleek enough.

There really is very little more to say on the subject of lines, except to impart one or two useful wrinkles.

It may be found very difficult to cast accurately at short range, even with the double-taper profile. This can be overcome by step-ping up the weight of the line one, or even two ratings. Casting depends upon the weight of the line actioning the rod, and if very little line is extended beyond the tip ring, then difficulties do arise. One way of countering this is to uprate the line, but great care must be taken not to forget that you have to all intents and pur-poses over-powered the rod for normal casting. Modern rods are pretty tolerant, but you should not expect miracles, and if you decide to make much longer casts, then you will have to change your tackle assembly. The use of a heavier line for very short-range work has absolutely no effect on the balance of rod and leader.

Fly lines are not cheap, and should be looked after with some care. At the end of a session, you should always rub the line down carefully to remove any trace of grit or mud, and never just wind it all back on the reel until your next outing. I do not think that a modern fly line wears out, no matter how much use it gets, but the plasticizer in the coating does tend to dissipate. This causes the line to stiffen up appreciably, and is followed quite quickly by cracks appearing, and failure to float. This can be avoided by replacing the plasticizer, and these days nothing could be easier. You buy a product named Permaplas and apply it to your line in accordance with the instructions. This replaces the plasticizer, and full flexibility is restored. In fact, a line treated in this way becomes quite as pliable as the old silk lines, and is much nicer to fish with.

An interesting point emerges here. When you dye your fly line, you are in fact not dyeing the line itself but the plasticizer that it contains. Thus, when your dyed line begins to look paler, it is an indication that the plasticizer is dissipating. In order to gain maximum line usage, you should now remove the line from the reel and re-plasticize and re-dye it before using it again.

There only remains the question of how much backing line you need to load on to your reel. If you are a pretty tough angler with good hands for playing a big trout, then you will rarely need as much as fifty yards, but for safety's sake, use not less than eighty yards and even then, keep your fingers crossed. With glass rods, I have experienced runs of up to one hundred yards before the trout could be stopped.

Of course everything that I have said in this chapter is relevant to fishing for all trout, not just the big ones. It may be that the smaller trout, being generally more naïve, will tolerate white lines, line flash, and casting which is neither accurate nor delicate. Big rainbows are not tolerant at all, and I insist that it is essential that every precaution must be taken against unnecessary creation of difficulties or hazards which will legislate against the really good fish being caught. By following the concepts outlined here, much of the risk associated with lines will be eliminated.

10 Fly reels and other accessories

Reels

I am quite unable to engender much enthusiasm for fly reels. Basically they are nothing more than a simple centre-pin, far too heavy, and have no purpose at all other than to hold line and interfere with the correct casting action of a fly rod. It would be infinitely preferable to be able to remove the reel from rod whilst fishing, and perhaps tuck it away in a pocket; but this would offer a major problem in the case of a fast-running fish and is therefore impracticable, more's the pity. If you take an average sort of fly reel, load it with eighty or a hundred yards of backing, and half a fly line, it can weigh anything from 10 ounces to almost a pound, depending upon the materials used in construction. And how about those fearful, clockwork-motor-driven so-called automatic reels, that have to be wound up like a toy train? I have never put one on the scales (because I do not like to touch them for fear of contamination) but I estimate the weight as being far more than I am prepared to tolerate. A man who can put one of those on a rod weighing 3 or 4 ounces, and cast all day, is strong in the arm but regrettably weak in the head.

Still, until some genius devises a totally new concept in fly reels, we just have to make the best of a bad job. All I ask of a reel is that it should hold enough line for my needs, not weigh a disproportionate amount, and should reveal a permanent disinclination to jam at awkward moments. I have several makes of reel which I find quite tolerable; the others I have given away to people I dislike. The Intrepid Gearfly range has certain merits, not the least being its ability to pick up loose line at a quite remarkable speed, and this tends to offset the disadvantage of minor excess weight resulting from the inclusion of a geared drive. Then I have a couple of ABU reels, the Delta 3 and the Delta 5, which have travelled around the world with me, and have never been so unkind as to offer me any mechanical problems at all. My biggest reel is the St Aidan, by Hardy Bros, and this has taken a tremendous amount of punishment over the years, in a singularly uncomplaining fashion, and although it is very shabby now, it is probably the sweetest of all my reels in the way it handles.

Do not make the mistake of thinking that a reel has any place in the playing of a trout. It is there to hold line, nothing more, and should never be permitted even to dictate the rate at which line is paid out, for the simple reason that a reel is normally less intelligent than a human being and is incapable of making the decision to amend braking power to suit varying circumstances. The playing of a trout has to be a manual process, in terms of the giving and taking of line.

Never let go of the line for a moment. The rod is held in one hand, with a finger or two available, if needed, to trap the line which is being dealt with by the other hand which is kept close to the rod grip. If you have to concede line from the reel, then it is the line-holding hand that dictates the rate at which it is paid out. In other words, when a trout is running, and all available slack has been given, then the line that is paying off the reel passes through the line-holding hand which imposes the required degree of braking.

In the recovery of line, similarly the reel plays no part. The spare fingers of the rod-holding hand are used to trap the line against the cork grip, while the other hand then pulls line through the fingers at whatever rate is indicated by the activity of the trout. If it is actually running towards you very quickly, it can be rather difficult recovering line manually at the required rate, but there is no way that a fly reel could attempt to keep up. All too many people feel that the 'right' way to play a trout involves disposing of loose line, and playing it from the reel. This is the best, and most efficient way to lose big trout that I can think of, offhand.

So what happens to the coils of line that you strip manually? If you are totally organized, and meticulous, you will allow them to fall into a line tray secured to some part of your anatomy. I cannot be bothered with this practice, mainly because the presence of another piece of equipment fastened to my person hampers my freedom to creep and crawl round, and through bushes, or wriggle along behind reedbeds.

My line is dropped in wide coils around my feet, and although this may sound an extremely dangerous thing to do, I can honestly say that has never hampered me from playing out and landing a big trout. I suppose the day will come when it will, but in the meantime I know that I would have lost a great many more had I attempted to play direct from the reel. I prefer to take the minor risk of a disastrous tangle, knowing that I still have the opportunity to control the trout on a short line, and retain the essential sensitivity of control bestowed by my manual system. *Chacun à son goût.*

Landing nets

The landing net is a very important piece of equipment, and one that usually has insufficient attention paid to it. Big trout require a big net, and not the glorified tea-strainer normally offered for sale as a trout net. The final decision on the net is subject to individual preference, but it should not be too dissimilar to those splendid nets usually described as specimen hunter's nets. You have to be

A big strong landing net ...

is a most ...

important item of tackle

able to encompass with it, a kicking, struggling trout that may range from 30 inches upwards in length, and with a girth of around 20 to 24 inches or more. You cannot fold these fish up to get them in. The net does require to be deep, and mine is more than 3 feet in depth, giving small opportunity for a leap to freedom. Handles are available in a variety of materials, and mine is metal, 5 feet in length, and capable of extension to 9 feet. It is heavy and, even dry and empty, difficult to lift left-handed. In use, of course, you never attempt to lift it very far out of the water. You sink it, draw the trout over it, lift it sufficiently to ensure that the trout cannot get out, and then drag it back through the water towards you very quickly, and up the bank. A professional strong man might, using two hands, manage to lift the whole thing vertically, but the net frame would collapse, and even the handle might break. I have seen it happen.

Knotless mesh is a very good idea, because hard knots can lacerate the trout and spoil its appearance, a quite unnecessary touch of avoidable cruelty.

I believe that an angler should always net his own fish, and if he does not, then he is not entitled to claim that he has caught it. Some fisheries do impose such a ruling, with offenders being expelled from the fishery. Quite right too. Besides, a good many trout are lost at the net, and what do you say to the dear old friend who has just made the error that lost you the trout of your lifetime? It just is not worth it; net your own trout.

Other accessories

Once you have dragged the net up the bank, well away from the water, kill the fish before you do anything else at all. Priests are easy enough to make, or cheap enough to buy, so have one available and use it immediately. The new designs of priest that contain a marrowspoon concealed in the shank are aesthetically quite pleasing, and work very efficiently. I must confess to lack of interest in the marrowspoon though. I do not need to know what the big trout I have just landed has been chomping; all I need to know is that it had just chomped the fly that I offered it. Later on, when performing the traditional disembowelling, I will be able to investigate dietary preferences in far more detail by examining the whole of the stomach contents.

Author with 16 pound rainbow

The fly has to be removed, and if it is small, or well inside the mouth, fingers will prove far less efficient for the task than artery forceps, which possess the excellent facility of locking on to the shank of the hook for manipulative purposes.

Weighing should take place without delay, because these big trout are capable of tremendous weight loss, even as much as two pounds in a day in spite of low temperatures. On a hot day, losses are even higher. A good-quality spring balance is ideal for a quick approximation of weight, although it should never be assumed to be accurate. At least you will know whether you should immediately cart the trout off to the fishery manager for immediate weighing as a potential fishery or British record.

When you think about it, you really do not need very much more in the way of accessories than these items.

Most of the tackle needs to be carried in some form of bag, and the Bob Church design is excellent, because his bag is quite large enough to take all the tackle required during a day's fishing (half a dozen reels, spare spools, four or five wooden fly boxes, two spring balances, cast wallet, etc., etc., etc.) plus adequate space for flasks and sandwiches. Mind you, this is far too heavy to be carried around the fishery, so I generally leave it at a vantage point, together with spare rods, and transfer the essentials to the pockets of my fly-fishing waistcoat. I was only recently converted to the use of these waistcoats, but I would not want to be without one now. Nine decent pockets, lambswool patches for used flies, ring for landing net (I use it as an anchor point for the cords that are attached to my priest and a knife), and all manner of other design points means that one takes one's house on one's back, as it were. This is yet another Bob Church design, and a superlative design it is too. Mind you, there is a big scarlet label that bears the name 'Garcia' in white upon it. I conceal this behind a badge of some sort, in case anyone thinks it is my name! Maybe I'm unduly sensitive.

Tucked away in a waistcoat pocket there is always a bottle of Permaflote, and a small pill-box containing a sort of putty made from mixing Fullers Earth with neat washing-up liquid, marvellous for de-greasing leaders.

Many people carry a small pair of scissors for cutting leaders. I still have my own teeth, and prefer to use them while they are still with me. I am not sure whether polarized spectacles are classified as an accessory, clothing or personal adornment, but you must have at least one pair, preferably two, against the time when you lose or break the first pair. Without them you will not see a fraction of what goes on under the surface, and your catch rate is bound to suffer. Buy the most expensive you dare afford; it will be well worth the extra cost.Cheap spectacles may have defective lenses which can give you a terrible headache as a result of eye strain.

No doubt everyone could expand on my basic list of accessories, but I like to think that I have given up non-essentials, and take with me only what could possibly be needed. I have taken this so far that I usually forget something important.

Harness

However odd it may seem, I feel that it would be wrong of me not to offer comment upon one further accessory which is now accompanying me on my travels. Basically, this is a light harness, designed to transfer the reel from the rod butt to the chest or abdomen of the angler, and is so simple in concept that I am surprised that no one has thought of it before.

Fine nylon webbing straps, fully adjustable, hold a pre-formed plastic moulding to the angler's body in any desired position. The moulding – mine is dark green and unobtrusive – is furnished with a Fuji quick-release reel seat, which grips the reel very efficiently. The line passes from the reel through the rod rings in the time-honoured fashion, and I find that no alteration in hand positions is necessitated by this variation in reel position. Indeed, since I invariably pursue the 'manual' system of playing a trout described earlier, the only difference that the use of this harness makes is the elimination of undesirable weight from the rod. This, in turn, simplifies casting and eliminates a great deal of stress from one's wrist.

Oddly enough, I have now learned how and why this mysterious concept of a reel 'balancing' a rod came into being. Years ago, rods were much longer and heavier than most of those in use today, and the leverage that such a long, heavy rod could exert on the angler's arm must have been considerable. Today, rods tend to be shorter and much lighter, the leverage is inconsiderable, and the balancing weight of a heavy reel is quite unnecessary as a general rule.

However, exceptions must be made, with reference to the physical make-up of the individual. For myself, I find that I can cast better, more comfortably, and with less strain when using this harness provided that the rods I am using are of lengths up to 9½ feet. At 9 feet 9 inches, I note that the advantages are largely negated, and there is little difference in performance in using the harness. With a rod of 10 feet – or more – the leverage exerted when the reel is removed from the rod is noticeable, and the effect fairly unpleasant and tiring. Of course, the point at which negation of effect is achieved must vary with the physical characteristics of the individual and it is probable that an angler with more powerful arms and wrists than my own could happily use a 10-foot rod without noticing inconvenience, while a smaller or less powerful man might feel stress with a rod as short as 9¼ feet.

The harness will require a great deal more usage and experimentation before it can be regarded as having proved itself, but I am sufficiently confident in its advantages to have had a 'special' made up for me. This is of larger size, to take a very large reel with six hundred yards of backing, and is being used in the pursuit of the smaller of the deep-sea big-game species. This is an interesting field of exploration, largely hampered in the past because the vast size of reel needed to hold essential backing has always interefered with the performance of the fly rod used.

11 Records and other matters

Anyone who has ever caught a really big fish of any species knows that it is impossible not to talk about it. I am no exception. Fortunately, it seems that many anglers really do enjoy hearing, or reading about such catches. I am fortunate that I have succeeded in catching a few fish which have broken one sort of record or another, and some of the experiences I have had may be of interest to others, not the least because they provide a further insight into my methods. Also, it has to be said, I have lost an important fish or two, and these experiences are also valuable, because they underline the sort of errors that one should try to avoid making, whether these errors are purely physical or are created by a fault in the reasoning processes. So in the hope that others may gain something from my experiences, or at least will be mildly entertained by them, I propose to retail a few anecdotes.

I should add that these anecdotes are completely factual, that no 'embroidery' has been added to improve the tales, and that the weights of the trout referred to as being caught are strictly accurate, and have all been subject to independent verification. Where a fish has been lost, the suggested weight is founded upon my own experience, plus the opinions of other very experienced anglers. There is no need for me to exaggerate the numbers or weights of the big rainbows that I have caught, although some angling writers have been sceptical about the pursuit of the very big fish. Over the years, most of these critics have been persuaded to concede that they were probably in error to offer these criticisms.

If I may go so far as to quote names, that superlative angler Brian Furzer had great doubts about the degree of skill necessary to catch big rainbows, but my standard comment that 'no one is really qualified to offer an opinion unless they have some factual experience of the matter in dispute' rather cut him to the quick.

Realizing that he was expressing opinion rather than fact, he promptly booked several day's fishing at Avington, and has been a regular visitor there ever since. I am sure he will forgive me for saying that he is still trying to catch his first 'double', and yet, this is an angler skilled and wily enough to achieve a place in the English international fly-fishing team.

Bob Church was another who had reservations, and in due course it became clear that Bob was being unduly influenced by the stories of big trout from one lake – or two lakes – in Hampshire, which were ridiculously easy to catch. They were badly conditioned, suffered from severe fin rot, and were perhaps within only a week or two from death when they were actually caught. I can sympathize with Bob; he had heard the stories about these old, half-dead trout, and assumed that all large rainbows were much the same.

Nevertheless, Bob being a scrupulously fair person, thought that he ought to investigate further, and he too found out that all was not quite as he had been led to believe. I am sure he will not mind my saying that he blanked out on his first day, but succeeded on the second day in landing his biggest-ever rainbow up to that time, weighing 8¾ pounds. He freely conceded that there was more to this type of fishing than he had thought. The opinion of a man like Church carries a great deal of weight, and it is not surprising that other very fine anglers like Dick Shrive, Peter Dobbs and Peter Stone felt inclined to investigate the matter for themselves. They were also obliged to admit that there was no easy route to success, and that any other assumption was entirely erroneous.

So the word has spread.

What are records?

The idea of records is generally misinterpreted. It is almost as if the captor of a record-breaking fish of any species has automatically to be elevated to a sort of angling peerage, to be attributed with a dazzling array of mystical powers and skills that are hopelessly beyond the reach of the ordinary angler. I suspect that this results from the confusion in the minds of many, when the term 'record' is used. Take the athlete who, by dint of years of training, self-sacrifice, and damned hard work, succeeds in breaking the record for the mile, or hundred metres. Obviously, such a person is worthy of high praise, should be fêted and honoured, given medals and toasted in the best champagne. Matters are rather different with fish. If you look at the records list, you will not see the names of the best anglers in the country therein inscribed. Instead, you will see a list of names that you have never come across before, and may never come across again: the unknowns, the average angler. Besides, it is the fish that breaks the record, not the angler!

What is truly important on that list of records is the weight of the individual fish, nothing else. We need to know that certain species of fish can attain certain weights, and at such weights can be caught on rod and line, because this increases our span of angling knowledge, and ensures that we are aware of the potential size of the species for which we choose to fish. If we are also told the detail of the tackle on which it was caught, it perhaps provides spin-off information about the sort of tackle rig that proved efficient on that day, or confirms our views on the quality of output of certain manufacturers. It also tells us, loud and clear, that the catch was made by Joe Soap, for whom luck held good to the point that his really rather inefficient tackle and tactics proved, on that one occasion, to be good enough to land a fish which, by a further overdose of luck, happened to be an ounce or two heavier than any other fish of that species officially confirmed as being landed previously.

Records *are* interesting, and catching record-breakers can be fun. So, in the interests of fun, I propose to tell you a number of my exploits which either resulted in the capture of a record-breaker of some sort, or, on the other hand, resulted in the loss of a fish which would probably have broken some sort of record, had I not allowed it to escape. It is possible that some information may be imparted as a result of the telling of these tales but I will be more than happy if I manage to provide some interest and amusement by these accounts. If I list the events sequentially, there may also be the concealed bonus that the reader may be able to trace over that period of time covered, the changes in my personal approach to this branch of angling upon which I am so thoroughly hooked.

Avington, 1975

During June of 1975, we enjoyed some quite delightful weather. Bright sun, blue skies, not a trace of wind; marvellous for the holiday-maker, but rather a drag for the trout fisherman, who, if he reads the traditional books, knows that he needs a fair amount of cloud in the sky, and enough wind to produce a nice 'lop' on the water. Fortunately, big rainbows do not read the same books as anglers, and hence they can be quite willing to be caught when the sun is up and the wind down.

On such a day, I was fishing at Avington, in my usual way – which means that only 1 per cent of my time is actually taken up with casting a fly, whilst the remainder is spent looking for something to offer that fly to. Time passed in this pleasant and unremarkable way, and then, during the very late morning as the sun was reaching its maximum elevation, I noticed a large trout moving in what I had already identified as a potential feeding area. Rather like the White Rabbit in *Alice in Wonderland*, this trout was obviously late for an engagement, and whizzed round and round in an irritated manner, as if it was trying to remember what it was that it had left somewhere, and needed urgently. It certainly did not need any of the black buzzer pupae that were hanging around just below the surface, waiting for something interesting to happen. Obviously, timetable pressures were too great to be bearable, and off went the trout even faster than it had arrived.

In much more leisurely fashion, I picked up the smaller of my ABU rods, tied a size 10 black buzzer pupa to the light leader, applied a lick of nail varnish to the knot, and put the rod down again. I smoked a cigarette or two, and then back came the same trout, in an even greater hurry and worse temper than before, made several more circuits of inspection, and rushed away again in a terrible rage. I took this as a signal to check my tackle thoroughly, testing every knot, and using a slip of stone to enhance the point of my hook, which may – or may not – have required that small attention. It never does any harm, and passes the time quite pleasantly.

Then the trout returned once more, but this time there was a great difference. The pace was leisurely, the mood jovial, and from the way that the buzzer pupae were delicately sipped, one after another, it was obviously time for tea. By the time the third pupa had been eaten, my imitation was lined up with the others. I tensed as it was given close inspection, but relaxed again as it was rejected as unsuitable fodder for any self-respecting trout. I left it there, but on the second circuit the trout obviously took offence at it, and sheered off. I took the hint, withdrew it, and tied on another version of the same thing. This received exactly the same treatment, as did the next five or six changes.

In desperation I forced myself to go through the motions of changing to a lighter leader, and tying on a size 18 pupa in hot orange – all the time willing the trout to stay around and continue to feed. Out went the tiny orange speck; the trout took one look at it, opened its mouth and positively gulped it down.

I pulled the hook home, and immediately the trout took off. I was scared to use too much restraint, even though line was stripping off the reel at a worrying speed. All the line went, then the backing started vanishing too, and I could clearly see the drum of the reel before I was able to call a halt. Patiently I worked the fish back from the far end of the lake, and just as impatiently it charged back there again. This went on and on, until at last the runs got shorter and shorter, although they still seemed as speedy, but eventually the fight was restricted to the clear area in front of me. Fifty minutes exactly after I had hooked it, the trout was on the bank. My tiny hook was still firmly embedded in the jaw, and there was no sign of the hook-hold having loosened at all.

Sam Holland weighed it very carefully, but could not get a higher reading that 13 pounds 1 ounce, which was an ounce below the then record. When the scales were checked by the Weights and Measures people, an underweighing error of 2 ounces at that weight was noted, so in fact my trout was an ounce over the record. About five weeks later, Julian Farmer landed a splendidly conditioned rainbow of 14 pounds 6 ounces, so that the odd ounces' variance on my trout became purely academic.

Avington, April 1977

During the winter months, Sam Holland decided to hold a rather special opening day on 1 April, and to invite a number of the 'deadliest' trout anglers in the country to try their skills against his trout, before less skilful anglers succeeded in putting them down for the rest of the season. On the day, those present were Richard and Patricia Walker, Bob Church, Peter Thomas, Peter Dobbs, Dick Shrive, myself and John Wilshaw of *Angling Times*. John brought Bill Goddard with him, undoubtedly one of today's finest fishing photographers.

The day was very poor, weather-wise. The wind was quite strong, gusting from all points of the compass, and occasionally bringing rain squalls with it. The water in the lake was not as clear as one could have hoped, and visibility was worsened further by the wind and rain. It was difficult to decide what to do for the best, but since the wind decided to settle briefly for a constant direction, I opted to fish the bank that had the wind heading diagonally into it. Peter Dobbs took a stance to my left, and Bob Church moved in on my right, leaving sufficient space between us for comfortable fishing. I studied the gravel banks which were quite innocent of weed down to a scarcely visible depth of six feet, and was convinced that I could see an occasional great shape cruising slowly down on the gravel, which is what I had anticipated having regard to time of year and wind direction.

I tackled up two rods, the RW Superlite with an 8-pound leader and a leaded Mayfly Nymph, and my new 9½-foot carbon-fibre rod loaded with a leaded Damselfly Nymph. It is worth adding that these dressings had been specially tied for me by Richard Walker, who had presented them to me the previous evening. Pete Dobbs was the first to feel the power of a big trout, and after a hectic battle he landed a fine 11¼-pound rainbow, in immaculate condition. I was the next to score, and this was on the Superlite and Mayfly Nymph. It took a very long time to subdue that trout and bring it to net, and as I recall, it needed three changes of rod from hand to hand, before it was beaten. This was a little bigger than Peter's, and tipped the scale at 11 pounds 14 ounces. Bob Church was next, and this was the fish that stripped line from his reel at an incredible speed, really bewildering him with sheer pace. Bob is too old a hand at the game to be beaten by speed alone, and he too netted his fish; it weighed an exciting 15½ pounds, and was without the slightest doubt the best-proportioned rainbow I have ever seen, and incredibly silvery and glittering.

Things went quiet for a while, and then I dimly saw another shape cruising slowly, down deep. I offered the Mayfly Nymph, once, then again, but the trout was not interested. I switched to the carbon-fibre rod with a Damselfly Nymph, and this was taken quite casually by the trout as I bumped it along the gravel in front of its nose. This was another dour battler, but I was delighted at the performance of the carbon-fibre rod which seemed to permit me to put more pressure on the trout, and kill it very much faster than the first, although it weighed a satisfactory 13 pounds 7 ounces.

I was quite tired by this time, and conditions had now worsened to the point tht trout were no longer visible, and since I do not like fishing blind, I strolled off the fishery and cadged a cup of coffee from Roy Ward, Sam's manager. I told Sam that I had caught two doubles, and asked whether I might stop fishing because of fatigue. Sam reacted to this suggestion in his usual forthright manner, and drove me – with hard words – back to the lake, where I was just in time to see Richard Walker latch into a hard-fighting trout which he soon brought under control in his usual smooth, efficient manner, and which proved to weigh exactly the same as my first fish.

Things were fairly quiet, so I took the opportunity to prowl the banks in search of a bigger trout than any yet caught, and also stopped for a gossip with Peter Thomas who was efficiently catching fine trout, but not getting to grips with the biggest. Dick Shrive had turned a big one over on the surface, but had the bad luck to see the hook come loose, and Pat Walker was stalking a monster lurking around a rather deep hole. Bob Church was also on the move, and so was Walker by this time, and we finally settled down again in our new positions with Church to my right again, and Walker on the opposite bank.

I took quite a long time checking my leader, retying the fly, and just watching subsurface activity. Then I saw a fine trout roll at the surface, a quite unusual happening, and I was in process of winding up to a speculative cast when I realized that the trout already had a big nymph in its mouth, from which a leader extended in the direction of Walker, who had, I now observed, a decided bend in his rod. He duly landed his second double of the day, a plump 12-pounder.

Eventually I saw another trout well worthy of a cast, since it was the biggest I had seen, and after a couple of refusals, the induced-take retrieve proved its undoing, and I was fast to a very powerful trout which swam with horrifying power to my right. Looking across to see that there was no obstruction which need concern me, I was very worried to find that Church was retrieving his line slowly, and my trout appeared likely to entangle itself in his leader. I called to Bob to move his line, realizing as I did so that I was wasting my breath, because there was no way he could react fast enough to the situation.

I had two choices open to me. I could do nothing, and hope that the tangle would not be serious, or I could clamp the brakes on hard, and try to stop the trout before it hit the trouble zone. I took

Author nets 18 pound 7 ounce rainbow, watched anxiously by Bob Church

the latter option, clamped the line between fingers and cork grip, and hung on for grim death. Too hard! Too late! The leader broke! It is always the one that escapes that is the biggest, I suppose, but I really did believe that trout to be the heaviest I had ever hooked up to that time. It was nobody's fault but my own, and looking back, I might have been better advised to let it run and risk a tangle. With an angler as good as Church on the other rod, I might well have got away with it.

At this point I changed my leader for a new one, and sat watching while Walker hooked into another very big fish that, untypically, he failed to land, the hook coming unstuck.

Time passed, and I eventually located another fine-looking trout which completely ignored a Damselfly Nymph, no matter how it

Author with 18 pound 7 ounce rainbow, temporarily the UK rod caught record

was presented, but on switching to the Mayfly Nymph, it was accepted on the drop. I saw the mouth open, and close, and my nymph had vanished. A firm pull anchored the hook, and I was fighting a very dour trout indeed, which pulled very heavily in spite of the fact that it did not seem to be of any very great length. It performed all the usual tricks of these dour fish, but I managed to keep the upper hand. To be honest, I was treating it in rather cavalier fashion, and if I had made just one mistake, I would have lost it. Fortunately, I made no mistake and succeeded in netting it and hauling it up the bank, whereupon my legs gave out under me and I sat down with a bump, feeling as if I'd been put through a wringer. Church came over to me, and stood there saying something about the depth of the fish, but it did not register for a while.

Then I looked, blinked, and looked again. What a fish! It was incredibly deep in relation to length, and very thick across the shoulder. Bob kept urging me to weigh it, and eventually I recovered my senses sufficiently to get a spring balance out. Something over 18 pounds it weighed, according to my balance (which always under-registers). So, picking up the trout, I staggered wearily back to see Sam, and have it weighed officially. Sam was not there, so I deposited the trout, which by now seemed to weigh a ton, in a cool spot in the hatchery, and cadged another coffee from Roy. Eventually I recovered sufficiently to return to the lake, but I had insufficient energy left to start fishing again.

Some three hours later, Sam appeared with the news that I had broken the British record again with that last trout, and that it weighed a splendid 18 pounds 7 ounces. It seemed too good to be true.

I was not allowed to rest, because everyone was urging me to get fishing and complete my limit with a fourth double-figure fish. I was reluctant, but allowed myself to be persuaded. It was silly, really, because I was far too tired to be competent, but I made the effort. Needless to say, I did not see another big trout, and eventually settled for a 4½ pounder.

Dick Shrive had worked the oracle by this time, and produced a lovely trout of around 13 pounds as I recall, taken on a Pheasant Tail Nymph, fished to an observed trout.

So ended possibly the most incredible day's fishing ever experienced. Bob Church had a 15½-pounder; Peter Dobbs had one of 11¼ pounds; Dick Shrive had a 13-pounder; Richard Walker had two for a thrilling 23 pounds 14 ounces; and I had three for 43¾ pounds. With the fourth fish, I had completed my limit with a total weight of 48¼ pounds.

It took just under a week for another double to be taken from Avington, and the successful angler took one and three-quarter hours to land a superb 19 pounds 2 ounces of hard-fighting rainbow, which took him all round the lake, and pulled him in the water for good measure. I had not even had time to apply for a form on which to make a record claim!

Church Hill Farm Fishery, April 1977

Because I was fishing at Avington on 1 April, I was unable to attend the opening of this new fishery, but had promised to go

Left to right: Author, Bob Church, Peter Dobbs, Dick Shrive

along the following day. I had planned to arrive at the official start time of 9 a.m., but the events of the previous day had taken their toll, and it was closer to noon by the time that I arrived, and there were a good many other anglers on the water, but none of them, surprisingly, in the area that I had envisaged as a potential hot spot.

This was in the vicinity of the feed-in to the lake, rather shallow, and with obstructions in the form of a tree stump or two, and some accumulations of twigs and branches. I settled myself comfortably, and on studying the water, noted some large black buzzer pupae in the margins. I tackled up with a 4-pound leader and size 10 black pupa, tested my leader with care, and continued just sitting and looking. Ten minutes or so passed without event, and then I could hardly believe my eyes when I spotted a large, portly trout, saun-

Airborne rainbow of 10 pounds 7 ounces at Church Hill Farm

tering along the shallows, picking off every black pupa in sight. I
cast as delicately as I could, and the fly landed four or five feet in
front of the trout, which continued to advance at the same leisurely
pace. It reached my artificial, and without pausing, sucked it in,
and closed those fat white lips. I pulled the hook home, there was a
quick flurry, and the trout was making determined attempts to
reach the tree stumps. I prevented this, not without difficulty, and
then had to mount a similar defence to prevent it boring into the
tangle of branches. It tried head-shaking, tail-flailing – all the standard ploys, but in gratifyingly short order, I had it on the bank. The
official weight proved to be 10½ pounds of very pretty rainbow,
and I had set another fishery record, which lasted for three weeks
until I myself broke it with another rainbow just 7 ounces heavier,
fishing the same area and using the same tactics and tackle. Even
the fight was a carbon copy of the first.

Avington, May 1977

This was rather a special outing, because I had been asked by *Angler's Mail* to undertake an exercise for them. It seemed that Ray Mumford, that great coarse angler and match fisherman, had expressed the wish to accompany me to Avington for a day's trouting, and the staff of the *Mail* thought it just possible that a picture feature might emerge from the session. I felt rather as if I was on rather a hiding to nothing, because I had to try to get Ray into contact with a decent trout, and yet he had only taken up the sport a few short weeks earlier.

Ray and I had a long telephone conversation before the great day, and my confidence was in part restored when I discovered that he had been practising his casting like mad, and was reasonably confident of his ability to be accurate at close range. And, of course, he has caught some very large coarse fish too.

We met at the fishery, Ray, Melvyn Russ of the *Mail*, and myself, about half an hour before we were allowed to start fishing, which gave me the chance to impress upon Ray the need to cast to a trout that he could see, the importance of a slow, slow retrieve, and how important it was to hustle and bustle a hooked trout, in order to gain the initiative from the outset. I asked the others to let me go down to the fishery first, and then to follow quite slowly in the hope that I could locate a trout for Ray by the time they arrived. In fact, I did better than that. I found two! They were both within close casting distance from the bank, clearly visible, but I gained the impression that one was takeable, the other not.

To expand slightly on this, one of the trout was resting in the partial cover of a small weed-bed, and appeared fairly comatose, possibly recovering from a prolonged bout of over-eating. The other was poised between mid-water and the lake bed, with fins quivering and a general appearance of bright alertness, obviously eyeing the corixae which were showing here and there. To test this, I cast to the likely one, and hurriedly withdrew my offering when a take appeared imminent. Several casts to the other indicated the correctness of my original surmise, because I could not induce even a glimmer of interest.

By this time, Ray and Melvyn had arrived. I pointed both the trout out, and suggested to Ray that he start work on the one most likely to take. He tied on a corixa imitation, and after he had tried a cast or two. I found myself very impressed with his accuracy and delicacy of presentation. The only mistake that he was making was the mistake that almost everyone makes; that of retrieving much too quickly. I nagged him soundly on that subject, watched one more cast, and then quite deliberately walked away, up to the other end of the lake. I had it in the back of my mind that there are far too many unpleasant people around, who would be likely to suggest that I stuck the hook in a trout for Ray, just so that he could claim the honour of the catch. I was sure that Ray would catch that trout, and I was equally sure that I wanted to be somewhere else, talking to someone else, at that time.

And that is exactly what happened. I reached the far end of the lake, talked to another angler for a moment, tried an experimental cast at a fair trout that was sticking its head out from below a raft of floating algae, and only then did I look back at Ray. His rod was very thoroughly bent! I walked back along the far bank, and as I reached the point exactly opposite him, he completed a very neat netting. What a fine trout! Sam Holland duly weighed it in at 16 pounds 6 ounces, and the main purpose of the trip had been accomplished.

Of course, I had to spoil it!

I spent several hours wandering around the fishery, in search of something special, but in fact spending most time talking to other anglers. At about three o'clock, I was standing back from the water's edge, talking to Melvyn and keeping a feeding area under observation, when I saw a very fine trout moving in. I pointed this out, checked my leader, and cast my fly as accurately as I could. Just at the second when fly and trout met, a heavy gust of wind rippled the water obscuring my vision, although I thought I saw the trout open and close its mouth. There was not even a quiver of movement from the line, so I merely waited patiently. The ripple died away, and there was my buff Pheasant Tail Nymph exactly where I had put it, but the trout was a yard further on. I cast again, and again came that infuriating gust of wind, but this time I was in a slightly better position, and retained partial vision. Again that great, white-lipped mouth opened, and this time my nymph was taken.

No sooner was the hook home, than the trout was off, speeding up the lake like a powerboat. I applied continual braking, and stopped it within thirty yards. Reluctantly it came back, then away it sped again, and again I stopped it at thirty yards. Once more this happened, and then the tactics changed. First of all, the trout tried to bulldoze its way into a reedbed, and every time I managed to turn its head away by massive sidestrain, it somehow or other found the extra strength to turn back again. Finally it gave this ploy up, and, boring straight down into a deeper hole, began flailing the line with its great spade of a tail. Thump! Thump! Thump! No tackle would stand that treatment for long, so laying the rod parallel to the water, I again applied very severe sidestrain. This pulled the line away from the trout; the flailing continued for a moment, but that damaging tail was no longer connecting with the leader, and finally I rolled the great fish over.

Now the fight was carried to another region, and, breaking surface, the angry trout began head-shaking tactics, facing me with its head clear of the water, and shaking it violently from side to side. I could see my nymph nicely lodged centrally in the top lip, but I could also see a mental picture of its being ripped loose if I maintained the tension on the line. So I dropped the rod tip, minimizing the risk, and very quickly the trout turned, and bored deep again.

Now it headed for a mass of algae on the bed, and although it made repeated attempts to seek refuge there, I found it fairly simple, if nerve-racking, to forestall this move. Then, very quickly, it changed direction, and bored into a clump of weed close at hand. This took me completely by surprise, but fortunately it was new growth, not very dense, and so soft, that the leader sheared straight through it without check.

Now the trout became more sluggish, boring deep, and temporarily another gust of wind obscured my vision. When all was clear once more, I saw to my horror, that the trout was hugging the bed very closely, and quite deliberately rubbing the hook to and fro on a gravel bank. I applied strain from all directions, but the fish was quite immovable. Now I was worried. I said to Melvyn, 'I'm going to lose this fish if I can't get it away from that gravel!' He nodded his agreement, and I continued to work on the trout, but without making the slightest impression. I felt that time was running short for me; the trout was now working faster and faster, stirring up a cloud of sand and tiny stones.

No matter what I did, the chances were now very great that the fish would beat me, and the time had obviously come for taking a risk which I would not normally have considered. I tucked the butt of my rod into my groin, applied maximum strain so that the rod bent alarmingly, and then suddenly dropped it, gained an inch or two of line, and heaved once more. This, as you know, is termed 'pumping', and is normally used to gain line on a big fish when one is using either a fixed spool or a multiplying reel. One *never* treats a trout in such fashion! For a while it was deadlock, and then I began to gain line – inch by inch that great trout came up to me, plunging and fighting like a demon. I slipped my net into the water, not in any great hopes that I would need it immediately, but just to have it ready.

Now I had lifted this incredible fish to mid-water, and there matters rested for a while. I was unable to gain line, but there was no way that I was going to cede any, either. Then at last the murderous pressure began to tell on the trout (I was running with sweat, and gasping for breath myself). Up, up, it came, and I rolled it over on the surface, beaten. As I drew it over the rim of my net, a puff of blood broke from its gills,and the battle was over. I looked at my watch to see how many hours the fight had been raging. Exactly nine minutes! I could not believe it.

As I looked at the trout lying there on the bank, bright silver and superbly proportioned, I knew immediately that this was the big one, that I had done it again. As I collapsed in a heap on the grass, I said to Melvyn, 'There's the new British record,' and Melvyn and Ray – who had joined us by this time – nodded their acceptance.

An hour or so later, the weight was officially confirmed at 19½ pounds; not only a new British record but a new World 'All Tackle' and 'Leader Class' record also. Nine minutes may not sound long to land such a hard-fighting fish as a big rainbow of close on 20 pounds, but believe me, it was a lifetime. I 'leaned' on that trout to a remarkable degree, treating it very roughly indeed, because I quickly reached the conclusion that the only way I was going to win was by brawling, carrying the fight to the trout, and not ever letting up on the pressure. I *thought* I was using an 8-pound level leader bloodknotted to a 10-pound extension, but I was hopelessly wrong about this because of a stupid mathematical error in converting metric breaking strains. Believe it or not, since I discovered that fact, I have had a severe attack of the shakes. I was very fortunate that my carbon-fibre rod was sufficiently toler-ant to be able to cope with the lighter leader, and still achieve an apparently perfect balance.

Author with UK and World Record rainbow of 19½ pounds

Avington, June 1977

I paid two visits to Avington during the month of June. On the first visit, I located a very large trout – certainly not less than 20 pounds – on a patrol which covered a fair amount of territory. I stalked, waited, and at last it began to feed very close in to the bank, in quite shallow water. This was a 'shrimper', taking the shrimps as they popped out of a small clump of weed, and on my first offer, it showed such great interest in my imitation, that I *knew* beyond all doubt that it would take on the next offer.

I was standing quietly checking my leader over before I re-cast, when a short fat man rushed up to me, splashed into the water between me and the trout, looked straight up at me and began a tirade in a charmingly lilting Welsh accent about having been on the water since nine o'clock butty, and not having seen one trout, isn't it? and are there any out in front of you, boyo? I looked ruefully at the mudstain that signalled the speedy departure of the trout that I was just about to catch, and said in my ugly English snarl that yes there blanking well had been a blankety blank trout out in front of me, but that it blanking well wasn't there any blanking more because some blanking Welsh twit had jumped in the blanking water, and scared the blanker away. I do hope that I caused no offence, but he left without another word.

A couple of weeks later I was back again, in the company of Bob Church, Dick Shrive, Reg Herbert and Ray Riley. It was not an easy day by any means. The fish were there in plenty, but knew all about anglers and their wiles, with the result that blanks were not uncommon. I found two big trout during the day. The first, possibly a 15-pounder, accepted my nymph with gratitude, and retired immediately to the middle of the largest clump of floating algae imaginable, to digest it. And, as far as I know, he is there still.

A little later, Riley called out to me that a huge trout had passed him by without a second look, and was moving slowly in my direction. I spotted it immediately, and after a moment to check the leader, made the cast of a lifetime. No trout could have been so ungracious as to refuse a nymph offered so precisely, and during the first few seconds of the fight, this obliging creature rolled on the surface under my very nose, in order that I should have no doubts about its size.

This was a canny opponent, because it kept setting off on fast runs, and then going through all the destroying tactics of tail-flailing, headshaking and bottom boring. It is difficult to counter these moves at long range, and for quite some time Dick Shrive on the opposite bank, and Ray Riley to my left, had a far better view of proceedings than did I.

I kept severe pressure on at all times, and after about twelve minutes the battle was over, and I began to work the exhausted trout back to me, along my nearside bank. The net was waiting, the trout was done for – and the hook came away about two seconds too early! Shrive said that he could see the trout, exhausted though it was, trying to rub the hook out on reed stems as I was bringing it back to me. Obviously it succeeded, and perhaps deserved to escape.

How big was it? Riley thought it must have gone over 25 pounds. Shrive thought the same, as did another angler who had a pretty good look at it. I was the only one who saw the fish broadside on, and I know to a pound what it weighed. I do not expect to be believed, but my best assessment is that it weighed between 29 and 30 pounds. I could have cried like a baby – still could for that matter. There is nothing I could have done to avoid the loss. A hook-hold giving way is beyond the ability of any angler to counter, and leaves one with a definite feeling of impotence.

Reactions to big trout

In the re-creation of these fishing days, there is one point that fails to come over very clearly, and that is my mental state from the moment that I first see a big trout to the moment that it is safely on the bank. Of course I am excited, wildly so, but I am perfectly able to contain that excitement and continue to behave in a calm, rational manner – quite unlike the reactions of a well-known angling writer who is a model of relaxation when playing a fish of 2 pounds or less, but, should he hook a larger one, behaves in quite a different way. His face alternates between purple and ashen, he points his rod straight down the line at the trout, and jumps up and down screeching 'What'll I do? What'll I do? Help! Help! Someone bring a net!' I am not making it up, believe me.

I look calm enough, but under the surface matters are very different. I am aware of a wild and desperate craving. I *want* that fish, I *must have* that fish; I would give up everything, sacrifice anything or anyone to possess that fish. It is almost as acute as a physical pain. And when the much-needed trout is on the bank, many people have remarked on the way that I seem to fold up, with white face and shaking hands. I know that this is true, but I also know that if ever that reaction failed to materialize, then there would be no point in continuing to fish. If that sheer need ever deserted me, then I would fish no more. Since there has been no change in more than forty years, I do not envisage that one will occur over the next forty.

People who need to ask, as many do, why I have this obsession with big trout, are usually quite incapable of comprehending my answer. Perhaps this is my fault, perhaps I lack articulateness, but I suspect that the fault is not mine alone, because there is always a follow-up question; 'What on earth do you *do* with a trout as big as that? Surely you can't *eat* it?

Photography

Well, I did have the 13 pound 3 ounce rainbow set up, but I doubt very strongly that I shall ever go to this trouble again. I am not enthusiastic about the trophy-gathering mentality, and a stuffed trout seems to lack any sparkle of life, becoming just a shabby, dusty and wrongly coloured replica – a sad relic of a heart-stoppingly exciting confrontation. Photographs are far better, particularly when taken soon after the event while the trout is still moist and glistening, *rigor mortis* has not yet set in, and the pallid face and sunken eyes of the angler – possibly overlaid with an expression of unholy glee – spark deep remembrances of the individual battles.

There is a tendency for modern photographic equipment to be brought into use which completely falsifies the appearance of size of the fish in relation to the angler. The inventors of the wide angle lens have much to answer for! With the irresponsible use of this item, trout are pushed forward at arms length, and appear in a photograph about as big as a whale about to swallow Jonah angler. Mind you, the angler's fingers are usually in view, looking like giant bananas, and this gives the game away very thoroughly.

Actually, the correct use of a wide angle lens does not falsify relative sizes. If the trout is held close to the body, in a normal relaxed position, it gains nothing in size, but does appear to

Author with 18 pound rainbow

The successful hunter. A two day catch of big rainbows totalling over 58 pounds

develop almost a three-dimensional quality, really standing out from the picture. Such photographs are worthy of being kept by the angler as a tribute to the quality of his catch.

What to do with big trout

Yes, of course I eat my big rainbows, and why not? A three-yearling trout weighing into double figures is a young fish, with tender, delicate flesh, and provided that it has been caught from a pure-water fishery, is possessed of a most delicious flavour. Normally, flesh colour is bright, deep red, comparable to the best salmon. In fact, some of the best recipes for cooking these fish are taken from salmon cookery books. It must be said that I have eaten so many trout over the years that I have tended to become a trifle bored with the flavour, and it is now fairly rare that I indulge myself with fresh trout. Instead, I send most of my bigger fish to the salmon smokers where they are smoked exactly as if they were salmon, and eaten in the same way.

A side of smoked rainbow is truly delicious, almost indistinguishable from smoked salmon, but just a shade preferable in flavour, and with a tenderness of flesh that requires the slices to be cut more thickly than salmon, in order that they do not fall apart. You, sir, with your 7-pound grilse. Why should you assume that your aged fish will be of better flavour and texture than my 12-pound rainbow of less than half the age?

My whole attitude is now such that my last record rainbow will remain, carefully wrapped, in the deep freezer, until such time as someone catches a larger. Then, without delay, it will go off to the smoker, and will be eaten with the utmost relish and enjoyment, by me, my family and my friends. After all, I am a hunter, not a trophy-collector, and the main purpose of a hunter is to provide the wherewithal to fill bellies.

12 Big trout of other species

Brown Trout

It may be thought odd that I have scarcely mentioned Brown Trout, because there is no doubt at all that brown trout are capable of reaching very large size, where their habitat is fertile and rich in natural foods. As I see it, the larger that a Brown Trout grows, the more likely it is to adopt a mode of life which requires it to spend most of its time in the very deepest water. You cannot really go in search of huge brownies; all that you can do is seek a technique that enables you to fish very deep water. For the greatest chance of success, the tackle should be a long line, armed with perhaps a hundred hooks, each baited with a whole herring, mackerel, or one-pound rainbow. This is rightfully banned on all fly waters. I know that the odd 10-pound fish is caught on a trolling lure attached to a lead core line, and that bigger ones are taken on trolled spoon baits, but I see little difference in principle between a trolled lure or spoon, and a static dead bait. Neither have the remotest connection with fly fishing.

Alpine Char

The Alpine Char (*Salvelinus alpinus*) is a very fine sporting fish which achieves weights in excess of 30 pounds quite easily, but unfortunately requires rather colder water than may normally be expected to occur in most of our trout fisheries. At one time, I had great hopes that the hybrid between this char and the rainbow, which is sterile and exceptionally fast-growing, could prove a beneficial addition to our game fish stocks, but again, in practice, it seems to require the colder environment in order to achieve its full potential.

North American Brook Trout

The North American Brook Trout, which is really another char (*Salvelinus fontinalis*), is a much more interesting proposition. Some stocks were imported into this country many years ago, but very little has been done to exploit its many advantages. The rod caught record stood for years at 2 pounds 9 ounces, and it has been a general assumption that this is only a minor species, not capable of being compared with brown or rainbow trout. Yet, the American record stands at 14½ pounds, and I have an unconfirmed report of another weighing exactly 1 pound heavier. This does not sound like a minor species to me!

I suspect that misconceptions have arisen here because very few trout farmers actually handle brook trout, and those that do seem to sell them on at quite small size for naturalization in waters which are usually large, or have a tendency to be deficient in natural food. There are a few lakes in Wales and Scotland where the species have become self-perpetuating, but few of these wild-bred fish are caught because they have adopted mainly deep water existence.

You may hear it said, sometimes by quite experienced anglers, that brook trout are free-rising, indiscriminatory feeders, far too easy to catch to have any attraction to the true sportsman. I can imagine two situations where these comments would be justified. If the fish are naturalized in an environment where food supplies are inadequate for the numbers present, growth rates will be poor because the fish will be starving, and they are likely to take anything that bears a remote resemblance to food. Also, in a fishery where far too many head of stock are introduced at any one time, until the stock density diminishes, there will be a major competition for anything apparently edible. This is as true of brown and rainbow trout as of brook trout. Where food supplies are plentiful, it seems not as easy to catch brook trout as it is to catch rainbows.

As an example of this, brook trout were introduced into Church Hill Farm Fishery at the rate of about fifty to the acre, and as a supplement to rainbow stockings of higher rate. This may seem to be a very high stock density, but is fairly common in the better of the small still-water fisheries. Also, depths run down to more than twenty feet, and the richness of the natural food supply would comfortably support more than three times that density.

At the end of the first month, only half a dozen brook trout had been taken, and I had caught four of these. Over the rest of the season, perhaps as many as twenty more were caught and retained, and I returned to the water quite a few more that were only lightly hooked. The catch rate for rainbows was many times higher, although stock density was only at most, twice as great.

Growth rate in this environment was exceptionally high; the faster-growing individuals doubling their weight in three months; a remarkable achievement.

Also, it was noted that sexually mature over-wintered fish regained prime condition much faster than rainbows. Not one black cock was seen during the early part of the season; all were in prime condition. Just one hen fish had failed to shed her ova, but there were none of the normal signs of stress attributable to this condition. The implication here is that in suitable waters, the brook trout may well offer advantages over the rainbow where residual stocks at season's end are anticipated, or where there is a requirement to over-winter a good head of stock.

The brook trout, like the rainbow trout, possesses a very large gene pool, which makes it an excellent subject for selective breeding programmes designed to achieve much faster growth rates. In America, it appears that several such breeding programmes have been adopted in the past, and fully documented results are available for study. In one such programme, it took just three generations of careful selection to produce char which, at a given age were twice the length of non-selectively-bred control stock Since the weight of a fish varies as the cube of the length, the new 'race' were eight times heavier than the control stock at exactly the same age, in spite of the fact that rearing procedures and environment were identical in every way.

There are people, sometimes apparently well qualified, who will state that it is impossible to improve stock by selective breeding, but there are very many scientific papers on the subject which prove conclusively in theory and practice the benefits of these breeding programmes. The rate of genetic change is directly proportional to the number of progeny of a mating, and in simple terms this means that the change that may be induced in prolific spawners such as trout in four generations would take bovine mammals at least 20,000 years to equal. If it was not possible to improve stock by selective breeding, horses would stand about twenty inches high, and our farm animals would be quite different from the high-yield creatures that we accept as the norm.

Since Sam Holland's rainbow programme is ticking over efficiently, he is now applying the Avington magic to brook trout, and results are proving very encouraging. I fully anticipate that we shall be enabled to fish for double-figure brook trout, and that these will be even more exciting than big rainbows. By 1980 we should know.

Tiger and Cheetah Trout

Not only big brook trout, but also big Tiger Trout and big Cheetah Trout will be available. What are these? The Tiger is the sterile hybrid of the brook trout + brown trout, and the Cheetah – which may well be quite extraordinary – is the sterile hybrid of the brook trout + the Avington race of rainbows. It may be wondered whether sterile hybrids such as these are of any interest to the angler. Quite a lot is already known about the Tiger Trout, because this is a hybrid which has already occurred naturally in this country, as a result of brook trout being introduced into an area in the Lake District. Here, they inter-bred quite freely with the wild brown trout, and the progeny was sufficiently numerous as to be remarked upon and correctly identified. In those far-off days it was known as the zebra trout, because of the pattern of stripes in its flanks.

It is an excellent game fish which takes savagely, fights like a demon, and because of its sterility, has an excellent growth rate, much faster than the brown trout.

The Cheetah Trout has an element of mystery about it, in that too few specimens are available for release into a fishery as yet, but it is known to be of extraordinarily fast growth, capable of tremendous speed through the water which, allied with normal heavy configuration indicates a powerful fighter, and also has excellent flesh quality. A fishery stocked with one or both of these hybrids need be subject to no close-season rules, because spawning is impossible.

Think of the financial benefits to a fishery enabled to remain open the whole of the year. I dare say that some will say that there is no fun in fly-fishing in the winter. They may be right, but stalwart salmon anglers appear to tolerate the cold, and whenever I attend press day at Packington, visibility is always obscured by heavy snow storms. That is just part of the fun.

To be fair, Tigers and Cheetahs are still very much a prospect for the future, but brook trout are with us today, and an increasing number of trout fisheries are including them in their stock.

Fishing for brook trout

The trouble is that any angler who wishes to find out more about the brook trout, and how best to catch it on a fly, is going to experience considerable difficulty, because there is a dearth of writing on that subject. Such books or articles as may be available tend to have originated in America, which can lead to difficulties in communication. For instance the Americans refer to the brook trout as a 'spec' which is an abbreviation of 'speckled trout', an alternative name. Then you have to understand the difference between a 'trophy spec' and a 'lunker spec'. The former seems to refer to a fish of about 5 pounds, and the latter to a larger fish of unspecified weight but presumably up to double figures.

If you plough through American writings, you will find a great many confusing terms and phrases, but if you refer to Damon Runyan, Dashiel Hammett, Raymond Chandler, Starsky and Hutch, and *Portnoy's Complaint*, you may just about see daylight. These days the fly is rarely used, and a spinner of some sort predominates, probably used in conjunction with a three-foot rod and an electronic fish finding gadget which 'gets you fish while your buddies are skunked'. Or something. Hand grenades for groundbait, I would not wonder.

I may still be proved wrong, but I made my own personal forecast, a couple of years ago, that brook trout were about to achieve prominence in this country, and I have been studying them carefully since I reached that view. For the first year, I had mainly to confine my attentions to farm stock ponds, but fortunately these were low-density natural ponds which encouraged a normal behavioural mode. This year, my scope has widened considerably, and I have been able to observe, and to fish for brook trout in several delightful fisheries. I have even managed to catch quite a lot, which I think allows me to offer some observations from a background of experience, specially since I have now thrice, broken the old UK record.

UK record brook trout of 4 pounds 8½ ounces caught by author in 1978

The brook trout is a handsome fish; the green marbling of the back giving place to dappled flanks with an iridescent bluish sheen, and a cream belly with orange-pink overtones along the keel. Pectoral and anal fins are reddish, with a white flash usually running the length of the second ray. The head is more pointed than the rainbow's, has a slightly underslung jaw well set with teeth, and the eyes appear to be set rather far forward, possessing the sort of mobility that is often associated with highly predatory species. Bodily configuration is pleasing, and the body depth, plus the breadth across the shoulder provides that high weight for length ratio usually associated with the old term, a 'well-proportioned fish'. This phrase has largely fallen into disuse, presumably because the angling public has become accustomed to the slim, immature stock fish of the reservoirs, and a correctly proportioned trout seems to be regarded as misshapen. By standards such as these, even a twelve-inch brook trout is a fat little fish, weighing rather more than brown or rainbow trout of identical length.

The predatory hints in the appearance of the 'brookie', as it is becoming familiarly known, are not belied by the pattern of behaviour that emerges in a study of the fish. More than most other game fish, it is an exploiter of the principle of ambush, and many points of resemblance can be drawn with those two coarse fish exponents of ambush; the perch and the pike, particularly the latter.

While it is still sexually immature, the brookie can frequently be seen in open water, suspended a few inches beneath the surface, quite motionless. If one can be seen, then careful survey will reveal that there are others distributed around the lake behaving in exactly the same way. This appears to be more common when the weather is mild, conditions quite bright, and water temperatures between the range of 13–20 °C. At lower or higher temperatures, it is less inclined to approach the surface, and appears to move to mid-water or deeper. During this static period, it seems virtually impossible to induce a take on the fly, and it is my belief that periods of heavy feeding are interspersed with these rest periods, which may have something to do with a requirement to digest food intake before feeding again. Suddenly, as if at a signal, all the fish under observation will begin to sink slowly down until they vanish from sight, and then a period of high feeding acitivity will commence. It would appear that the positioning of the eyes, and their high mobility, confer the advantage of extreme forward vision, and the brookie will make high-speed dashes to seize an item of food which may be several yards away, and, if this is close to the surface, the 'follow-through' is such that a typical oval rise form is created.

So within the context of the temperature range, brightness of the day, and size of the fish, the feeding pattern may be seen to be a series of very fast rushes until appetite is sated, followed by a totally static period.

I have noticed that these static periods can be affected by a change in the weather, and that a sudden shower of rain, or a heavy gust of wind, will also induce a slow drift to a greater depth, but unassociated with the start of a feeding cycle. During dull, cold, or wet weather, there is little surface activity, except perhaps during early morning or late evening, and it appears likely that the attention of the fish becomes concentrated upon bottom-feeding.

Although these smaller brookies can scarcely be said to adopt shoal habit in the classic sense, it may well be noticed that the 'spacing' they choose to adopt during the static period appears to be governed by a sense of territory, with each fish occupying an area of water roughly equal in extent. Of course, this does depend upon the density of stock, but is perfectly apparent at densities of thirty to the acre, and upwards. The fact that all observed brookies commence feeding at the same time also underlines a shoal habit propensity, and it may well be that in a still-water environment they form a shoal which is not as close as we would expect from the habits of our native shoal fish, but is spaced in accordance with some inherent territorial requirement.

As growth continues, it seems that the brookie becomes more fiercely territorial, and even the loose shoal ties vanish. The ambush tactic becomes a permanent way of life, and much time is spent lurking in places of concealment such as tangles of sunken branches, sparse growths of reeds or stems of other emergent plants. It is now that the marbling of the back and dappling of the sides comes into its own as a camouflage system. From such vantage points it makes lightning-fast forays to seize a food item, which may progressively be more likely to be small fry.

Just like the pike, the brookie seizes a small fish across the body, shakes it about like a dog with a rat, and often seems to return to its lurking place before turning the fish round and taking it head first. It appears that some of the most successful American 'lunker-hunters' locate the lurking places of big brook trout by trolling a very large vibratory spinner around potential holding spots, and once the fish's interest is aroused, substituting a much smaller spinner with which hooking is more likely to be achieved.

Even the smaller specimens take food fish crossways, and time after time I have watched them seize a lure in exactly the same way. There is a savage take, but since on a long-shank lure the hook point is normally outside the brookie's mouth, it is rare for permanent contact to be achieved, unless the point enters the outside of the jaw. An obvious answer to this is to use a tandem lure, but I find it just as effective to dress the lure to a short-shank hook, so that the point is about halfway along the length of the dressing. For the bigger specimens, the normal long shank can be used but the hair wing or streamer should be extended well beyond the bend.

I have enjoyed some success with tiny bugs, but so far the most popular body colour has been black, and the most successful pattern of all has also contained a small amount of white. It does not seem to matter how one introduces this white contrast, and the pattern I now use in preference to any other is a simple one. On a size 14 or 16 round-bend hook, create a very slim peacock herl body, as if tying an emaciated B and P Spider, then tie in at the head, a dozen or so white hen hackle fibres so that the tips just reach the bend. Finish with a neat head.

This should be cast out, allowed to sink slowly for a fair length of time, and then drawn back about a foot very quickly, after which it is allowed to sink again before the process is repeated. Takes usually come just after the fast retrieve is commenced, or, less frequently, at the end of the fast retrieve but before the nymph has had the chance to begin to sink again.

I have not had success with many lures, but there are two patterns which seem to be very killing. One is Mrs Palmer, described earlier, but it has to be the correct tying with a long streamer of pale yellow goat hair. The other is a dressing that I have never seen offered for sale in this country, the Palmered Parmachene. This has a tail of mixed red and white hackle fibres, a scarlet chenille butt, a white chenille body over-tied palmer-fashion with a white cock hackle. There is a hair wing, which should be longer than the hook, made up of three layers of bucktail or goat hair. The first layer is white, the second red, and then white again. The dressing is completed with a biggish black head, well varnished, and possibly a white eye with red pupil added to this can have merit. As a change fly, follow the above tying exactly, but substitute yellow chenille for the body.

It seems non-productive to strip lures very quickly, and I have enjoyed most success with a fairly slow retrieve and a pause between each pull. Takes are quite unmistakable, and a brookie of only 2 pounds will smash into a lure hard enough to jerk the rod tip round viciously, so it is not advisable to fish with too light a leader even though you do not expect to contact very large specimens. The problem is not in the playing of the fish, although they are fast and powerful, but in absorbing the shock of the smash take.

Matters are more difficult when conditions induce the brookie to feed deep, because one does not know whether to fish mid-water or bottom. Either can be productive, but generally I have achieved better results by fishing the lake bed, on a sinking line. Using one or other of the lures already described, cast out and allow adequate time for line, leader and lure to sink to the bottom. Keeping the rod tip very low, give a long, slow pull of about a yard; pause to allow the lure to settle again, and then repeat. At the final stage of retrieve, raise the rod tip high on the last pull, so that your lure appears to be darting to safety in the shallows. A take will often materialize at this moment, as the brookie sees its intended snack escaping, but in all fairness, it is quite difficult to gain a hook-hold, because the brookie is running at you very quickly, and frequently continues running right into the bank.

I have watched the behaviour of brookies in shallowish, clear water when fishing in this way. The lure as it drags along the bottom stirs up tiny amounts of mud or sand, and this seems to attract the attention of the fish, which will follow curiously, and more often than not, make a rush at it. The slightly underslung jaw formation seems to make it quite difficult for the lure to be picked up, and several such attempts may be made before the brookie succeeds, or loses interest. I thought it might be better if the lure was buoyant, and floated up off the bottom sufficiently to make the take easier, but this so far has proved quite ineffective, possibly because it is the mud-stirring effect that creates interest in the first place.

In waters where midge larvae – the bloodworm – abound, brookies will often be found stuffed to the gills with these tiny creatures. I have never yet succeeded in taking one on an imitation, no matter how good, although I have caught one or two on slim-bodied lures tied with scarlet body and sparse hairwing in the same shade.

When the time comes, as come it surely will, that the smaller fisheries begin to hold stocks of large brook trout in sufficient numbers as to make it worthwhile devoting time to their capture, I have little doubt that the anglers who are most successful will be those who have adapted big rainbow tactics to the special characteristics of this species. More than ever there will be the need to spend hours in observing the environment, identifying the ambush points, and locating the lurking brookie. We will have to learn to recognize, from external appearances, the fish which is in the static mode, and that which is poised ready for the killing rush as soon as food appears. Tackle balance will have to be given careful consideration; a leader strong enough to withstand the smash take, but fine enough not to cause alarm, and pliable enough to enable

Brace of brook trout – 4 pounds and 4 pounds 8½ ounces caught by author in 1978

effective presentation. The question has to be considered whether the projecting tooth structure will cause serious problems. Big rainbows, of course, have well-developed teeth, but they are set sufficiently far back not to cause too many problems as a rule. Brook trout teeth are something else again, as many a careless angler knows to his cost as he licks his wounds after attempting an incautious hook extraction.

I am hoping that time will show that the lure is not necessary for this species; that they can be taken consistently on good imitations of small natural food items, because otherwise I can see a serious conflict of interests arising between the various camps of big rainbows and big brook trout enthusiasts. It has to be remembered that many fisheries ban the lure, but such a ban would be very frustrating if this was truly the only effective dressing for big brookies.

Make no mistake, we shall have very big brook trout available for capture before too long, and equally certainly their introduction will cause problems and controversies. Nevertheless, I look forward to that time with keenest anticipation, and when the dust of dispute has finally settled, most sensible anglers will be delighted that the species of game fish available has been expanded by such a worthy opponent, such a tough fighter, and – it has to be said – such a superlative table fish.

Briefly, the Tiger Trout appears to follow a similar behaviour pattern to the big brook trout, tending towards a solitary, fiercely predatory mode of life. No official records exist yet for this hybrid, but unofficially the largest at the present time caught by fair fly-fishing weighed 2 pounds 6 ounces. For what it is worth, I caught it on a Palmered Parmachene.

No Cheetah Trout has yet been identified as being caught anywhere in the UK. This omission will surely be rectified before too many years have passed.

13 Conclusion

Looking back over the preceding chapters, I believe that I have made it clear that I do not believe that very big rainbows behave in the same way as small rainbows; that their feeding habits are far more restrained and selective; that they adopt a very territorial way of life, do not often diverge from their predetermined patrol and feeding routes, and rarely remain at rest for any length of time in any area other than their nominated rest areas.

Of course, angling is very like economics, in that both are very inexact sciences where 'laws' are nothing more than tendencies for things to occur in certain ways depending upon circumstances. Therefore, there is no 'always' in any branch of angling, no fixed pattern of behaviour or immutable sequence of events occurring in strict chronological order. One cannot plan a campaign against big trout where every move is calculated in advance, fully orchestrated and choreographed. Instead, one has to treat it like a jam session, where a musician improvizes a sequence of notes, knowing that however impeccable his improvizational concepts, he is still forced to work within a fixed framework of base key, accepted modulations and chord sequences, plus the predefined length of the original melody, and possibly even an immutable rhythmic pattern.

Thus the angler, as well as the jazz musician, appears to have total free will in what he does, and how he does it, and the more skilful that he is, the more free will he appears to possess. Nevertheless, no matter how wild and free the improvization, unless the basic rules are adhered to, the final result will usually be a total disaster. In this book, I have tried to define a basic set of rules, a framework of simple disciplines, which will allow the angler to catch big trout. This is not to say that the rules cannot be changed in accordance with personal preference, and additional or alternative guidelines established by reference to experience and logic. My own preference for light leaders necessitates the use of soft-actioned rods, and I believe implicitly that the very high success I have enjoyed with big trout is directly proportional to the fineness of leader used, in that the fly is permitted to work in a very natural manner, plus the benefit that a fine leader is far less visible than a heavy leader. Another angler may choose to use a heavier leader, and this will permit the use of a more powerful rod which in turn may lead to a higher degree of control over the trout and a reduction in the length of the fight. It is my own experience that, in heavily fished waters particularly, the net result will be that far fewer trout will be persuaded to accept the fly.

Similarly with all the other alternative guidelines I have investigated: I have found it preferable to discard them because they too legislate against the possibility of success. This is not to say that a better angler than myself could not make the alternatives work very satisfactorily, but I cannot have faith in, or recommend, techniques in which I am not competent and of which I suspect the conceptual validity. That would be dishonest.

It is intriguing that my systems can be used not just to catch very big trout, but also to catch the biggest trout in fisheries which lend themselves to the approach. If your favourite fishery is a small, clear stream where the average trout runs four to the pound and a big one weighs 12 ounces, you will find it quite simple to adapt the principles of observation and selection to assist you in evading the smaller fish and catching, on a more regular basis, the larger ones.

Frankly, there is ample evidence to show that the basic principles can be successfully adapted to fishing for many different species of fish, using tackle which appears in many ways to be totally unlike fly tackle.

And yet, I wonder whether it is really so different. Not too long ago I found myself boat fishing over the Challenger Banks off Bermuda. The tackle was IGFA 12-pound rating, a very light big game rod armed with a multiplying reel, monofilament line of 11 pounds tied direct to an eyed hook on which was impaled an anchovy. The quarry was Allison's Tuna, and by careful observation I was able to select the largest specimens of those in the vicinity, and successively offer them an anchovy in exactly the same way that I would present a nymph to a big trout. I caught both of those that I tried to catch, and they weighed 60 and 65 pounds respectively. None of the other fish would have weighed as much as half the weight of the smallest of the brace, but although all the tuna were zooming about in their usual excitable fashion, it did not prove at all difficult to select the largest, once observation had provided the essential data of preferred swimming depth and pattern of movement. Thus, although it seems improbable that trout and tuna have much in common, the basic principle of observation and selection remains constant, just as it does for all fish which are sufficiently cooperative as to allow the angler to study them in their natural environment.

Quite arbitrarily, I have defined a large rainbow trout as one that has attained or exceeded 10 pounds. This is a purely personal assessment – another angler might prefer to opt for 5 pounds, or 15 pounds, as the criterion. It may be that to some anglers, a weight of 10 pounds seems impossible of achievement, a target beyond their wildest dreams. A few years ago this may have been true, but nowadays an ever-increasing number of fisheries are stocking with a percentage of such fish, and I confess that I am greatly relieved that few of these are badly conditioned, worn-out brood stock nearing the end of their life cycle, remarkable only for their lack of ability to fight and an all-too-obvious scarcity of fins.

It is possible, I suppose that fisheries containing whoppers may still be scarce in certain localities, and that the specific angler may lack the inclination, or the transport facility, to journey far afield to such a fishery. In this case, I strongly recommend that the tactics, tackle and techniques defined in this book are utilized, with whatever minor adaptation might be required, for the extraction of above-average fish from any fishery where stock observation is feasible for at least part of the season.

The correct approach, allied with patience and persistence, will result in the capture of far more above average sized trout than can realistically be attributed to luck.

Lady Luck is a fickle goddess, and although we can all be grateful for her occasional and minor blessings, it is a foolish angler indeed who believes that consistent catching of big trout can be achieved by the traditional obeisances of throwing salt over the left shoulder, avoiding walking under ladders, knocking on wood, or raising one's hat to each and every magpie one meets.

Consistency in catching big fish requires hard work, discipline, and the exercise of imagination, too. This can be quite a burden, particularly if one has to start from scratch, since it is all too easy to develop an incorrect concept, a false foundation upon which to erect the edifice of endeavour.

This book summarizes my own endeavours and eliminates the false concepts which I developed from time to time. It summarizes the essential disciplines formulated over many years, which to date have enabled me to catch many more trout over 10 pounds than anyone else of whom I have ever heard, in this country, at least. If you follow my instructions, you ought to catch bigger and better trout too, and many of them. If, in due course, you catch more trout, and bigger trout, than I have been able to catch, no one will be more delighted than me. After all, it is the purpose of this book to assist you in achieving that very objective.

Appendix: UK fisheries capable of producing rainbow trout in excess of 10 pounds

All these are, at time of writing, day-ticket waters from which it is possible to catch rainbows in excess of 10 pounds. There are many other such fisheries of which I do not have sound personal knowledge and which therefore have been omitted.

Avington Trout Fishery, Avington, Winchester, Hants. (Itchen Abbas 312)

Church Hill Farm Trout Fishery, Mursley, Bucks. (Mursley 524)

Crown Netherall Trout Fishery, Hoddesdon, Herts. (Hoddesdon 61048 or 43013)

Stafford Moor Fishery, Dolton, Winkleigh, North Devon. (Dolton 360, 363 or 371)

Haldon Ponds, Exeter, Devon. (Craddock 40658)

Bradfield Ponds, Cullompton, Devon. (Craddock 40658)

Lower Moor Fishery, Oaksey, Malmesbury, Wilts. (Minety 232)

Argal Reservoir, Devon. (Kilkhampton 262)

Kennick Reservoir, Moreton Hampstead, Devon. (Exeter 50861)

Upper Tamar Lake, Kilkhampton, Devon. (Kilkhampton 262)

Willow Pool, Linch Hill Fishery, Witney, Oxon. (Standlake 774)

Exe Valley Fishery, Exbridge, Dulverton, Somerset. (Dulverton 23328)

Boringwheel Fishery, Nutley, Sussex. (Nutley 2629)

Leominstead Fishery, Emery Down, Lyndhurst, Hants. (Lyndhurst 2610)

Allen's Farm Fishery, Sandleheath, Fordingbridge, Hants. (Rockbourne 313)

Index